KT-579-124

◆ BRITAIN ◆
A COUNTRY REVEALED

Written by Sally Roy
Picture research by Alice Earle
Page design by Alison Fenton

Produced by AA Publishing
Copyright © Automobile Association Developments
Limited 2006

ISBNs 0 7495 4818 5 / 0 7495 4884 3
    978-0-7495-4818-6 / 978-0-7495-4884-1

All rights reserved. No part of this publication may be
reproduced, stored in a retrieval system, or transmitted in any
form or by any means – electronic, photocopying, recording or
otherwise – unless the written permission of the publisher has
been obtained beforehand.

Published by AA Publishing (a trading name of Automobile
Association Developments Limited, whose registered office
is Fanum House, Basing View, Basingstoke, Hampshire
RG21 4EA; registered number 1878835).

A02496

The contents of this book are believed corrrect at the time
of printing. Nevertheless, the publishers cannot be held
responsible for any errors or omissions or for changes in
the details given in this book or for the consequences of any
reliance on the information provided by the same. This does
not affect your statutory rights.

Colour separation by MRM Graphics Ltd, Winslow,
Buckinghamshire
Printed in China by C & C Offset Printing Co., Ltd

The AA's website address is www.theAA.com/bookshop

TITLE PAGE *A gateway to the Tudor mansion of Hampton Court Palace*
PAGES 2–3 *Terraced ranks of coal-miners' cottages in the Rhondda, south Wales*
PAGES 4–5 *Sea cliffs at Birling Gap, East Sussex*

Contents

London 8–19
Trafalgar Square and the Houses of Parliament 10–11
St Paul's Cathedral and Tate Modern 12–13
New London Landmarks 14–15
London's Markets 16–17
Buckingham Palace 18–19

Southeast England 20–39
The Sussex Coastline 22–3
Dover and Canterbury 24–5
Rye 26–7
Brighton 28–9
Bodiam Castle 30
Knebworth 31
The South Downs and Lewes 32–3
Portsmouth 34–5
The New Forest 36–7
Windsor Castle 38–9

Southwest England 40–63
Stonehenge 42–3
The Dorset Coast 44–7
Bath 48–9
Exmoor 50–1
Resorts of the Southwest 52–3
Gardens of the Southwest 54–5
Dartmoor 56–9
Clovelly and Brixham 60–1
St Ives 62–3

Wales 64–85
Cardiff and the Gower 66–7
The Brecon Beacons 68–71
The Pembroke Coast 72–3
Portmeirion and Porthmadog 74–5
Snowdonia and the Great Little Railways of
    North Wales 76–9
Anglesey 80–1
Conwy and Llandudno 82–3
The Vale of Llangollen 84–5

Central England 86–109
Ludlow and the Marches 88–9
Liverpool 90–1
Ironbridge 92–3
Oxford 94–5
The Cotswolds 96–9
Shakespeare Country 100–1
Cambridge 102–3
Wool Towns of East Anglia 104–5
Norwich and the Norfolk Broads 106–7
North Norfolk 108–109

Northern England 110–31
The Peak District 112–5
The Yorkshire Dales 116–9
York 120–1
North Yorkshire 122–5
The Northumberland Coast 126–7
The Lake District 128–31

Scotland 132–157
Edinburgh 134–7
Burns Country 138–9
Glasgow 140–1
Loch Lomond and the Trossachs 142–5
Iona 146–7
The East Neuk and Culross 148–9
St Andrews and Dundee 150–1
Around Glencoe 152–3
The Western Isles 154–5
Skye 156–7

Index 158–9
Acknowledgements 160

London

The capital of Britain, a vast metropolis stretching more than 30 miles (48km) to the north and south of the River Thames, London is Europe's largest and ethnically most diverse city. It dominates British national life, is the centre of law-making and the hub of the money markets. Its citizens see themselves as a people apart, with provincial life beginning where the city ends. Londoners have every reason to be proud of their city, an exciting and dynamic urban sprawl, whose confines contain world-class museums and galleries, historic buildings, magnificent churches and cathedrals, huge and verdant parks and gardens, and some of the best theatre, music, shopping and eating to be found anywhere in the world.

The city was founded as the capital of Roman Britain in 43BC, but its main expansion started after the Norman Conquest of 1066, when William of Normandy was crowned king in Westminster Abbey, and has continued ever since. Over the centuries London has sprawled to absorb scores of villages which once stood well outside its walls, and it's these that now form the wonderfully varied neighbourhoods of this culturally rich city.

Many districts are inhabited by descendants of the immigrants who have poured into London through the ages – in the last century alone, thousands arrived from the Caribbean, the Indian subcontinent, the Mediterranean and the Far East. Today, like the native Cockneys and Britains from all over the country who work here, they see themselves as Londoners, with a sense of historical and cultural pride in their unmatched city.

Chelsea Pensioners – army veterans residing at London's Royal Hospital, founded in 1681 – enjoying the afternoon sun

9

Trafalgar Square

From Parliament and the neighbouring Westminster Abbey – scene of every English coronation since the 11th century – Whitehall runs north to Trafalgar Square, designed by Charles Barry and John Nash and built between 1829 and 1841 to commemorate Admiral Lord Nelson and his 1805 victory against the French at Trafalgar. Surrounded by fountains and guarded by lions, a statue of the great man stands atop a 165ft/50m column, gazing benignly over the political demonstrations and public celebrations the square hosts each year.

The Houses of Parliament

Britain's laws have been debated at the Westminster parliament since the 16th century. Members meet in two chambers in the grandiose riverside building designed by Charles Barry and Augustus Pugin, after a fire in 1834 destroyed much of the older structure. The superb Westminster Hall, built in 1199 and topped off by Europe's largest hammerbeam roof, survived this fire, and is still used as a place of lying-in-state for monarchs and their consorts. For many visitors Parliament is synonymous with Big Ben, the 1859 clock tower.

BELOW *Trafalgar is one of the few London squares with fountains. They were completed in the late 1930s and are overlooked by the church of St-Martin-in-the-Fields, noted for its tradition of church and chamber music, and its care for homeless people*

LEFT *Behind the riverside terrace of the Houses of Parliament lie the debating chambers, flanked by Big Ben on the right. The Commons chamber, dating from 1858, was rebuilt after its destruction by bombing during World War II*

St Paul's Cathedral

In 1666 the Great Fire swept through the City of London, destroying acres of buildings, among them old St Paul's Cathedral. Architect Christopher Wren was commissioned to design a new one, along with 51 other City churches, and work started in 1675, continuing until 1711.

Distinctly baroque in spirit, the cathedral is surmounted by a massive classical dome, and fronted by two towers which flank the classically inspired entrance with its pediment and pilasters. Inside, this architectural set piece is lavishly decorated with carved wood, marble and gilding, seen at its best in the chancel and choir. Overhead soars the great dome, encircled by the Whispering Gallery, so called because of its acoustic properties – words whispered on one side are audible over 100ft/30m away on the other.

The nave is packed with monuments to the great, including an effigy of the metaphysical poet John Donne (c.1572–1631), one-time dean of St Paul's. There are more star names in the crypt, burial place of Nelson, Wellington and Wren himself, whose modest tomb is carved with a Latin inscription that translates as 'Reader, if you seek his memorial, look about you'.

ABOVE St Paul's and the Millennium Bridge viewed from the upper galleries of Tate Modern

Tate Modern

South across the river, and reached via the stylish Millennium footbridge, there's art of a very different kind at Tate Modern, where a vast international collection of 20th-century artworks is housed in the former Bankside power station. Tate Modern is the largest modern art gallery in the world, including works by artists as diverse as Monet, Picasso, Dalí and Mark Rothko, and its colleection is shown on a six-monthly changing rota. Works are displayed thematically rather than chronologically, giving a thought-provoking edge to the displays that's missing in many of London's older galleries.

The building itself is a brilliant conversion of an industrial space that has retained the sober atmosphere of the massive turbine hall, mainly used for cutting-edge installation art, while providing wonderfully light and spacious galleries on the upper floors.

OPPOSITE Trompe l'oeil frescoes by James Thornhill decorate the inner dome of St Paul's, high above Grinling Gibbons' beautiful choir stalls; he was also responsible for the superb organ case carving. The instrument has been played Handel and Mendelssohn

13

OPPOSITE *Giant wheels are a traditional way of celebrating the turn of the century, and the London Eye, on the Thames bank, draws visitors from all over the world*

LEFT *Passengers must board the capsules of the great wheel while they are in motion, then choose which direction to view*

BELOW *As much like a rocket nose as a gherkin, the Swiss Re building celebrates the best of modern architecture in the capital*

New London Landmarks

London may have officially marked the year 2000 with the ill-conceived Millennium Dome, but in the public mind, it's the London Eye, a giant observation wheel on the south bank of the Thames, that's synonymous with the turn of the century. Designed by the architects Julia Barfield and David Marks, the wheel, 443ft/135m high and containing 1,700 tonnes of steel, is the largest ever to be built, its 32 constantly moving capsules giving ever-widening views over London as they slowly rise and fall. The Eye has quickly proved itself both a favourite London landmark and one of the capital's most popular attractions. More than 15,000 people daily take a half-hour 'flight', which offers the unique experience of actually seeing the whole of this great city, some 25 miles (40km) across in every direction, spread around London's sixth tallest structure.

Across the Thames to the northeast rise more 21st-century architectural splendours – great towers of glass and steel that celebrate London's status as one of the world's premier financial centres. Among the most revolutionary is the Swiss Re Tower, affectionately dubbed the Gherkin by Londoners even before its completion in 2004. It occupies the site of the old Baltic Exchange, destroyed in the early 1990s by IRA bombing, and was designed by Norman Foster.

It's a fitting balance to Richard Roger's brilliant Lloyd's Building (1986) which rises to the south. That building's innovative interior, with its giant atria and rotating layout for each floor, and use of glass and steel, arc hallmarks of Roger's work, which can also be seen at City Hall (the bulbous glass GLC headquarters) across the river in Southwark.

London's Markets

The ethnic melting pot that London became during the 20th century brought an influx of food and goods from all over the world, and the city's markets, which attract tourists and locals in equal measure, are the best place to appreciate the vast range of food available in the capital.

Since the Middle Ages, London's wholesale markets – Smithfield for meat, Billingsgate for fish, and Covent Garden for fruit and vegetables – have supplied the city's needs in a frenzy of dawn activity laced with Cockney charm, which continues today. Covent Garden moved to an unglamorous site south of the river in 1973, but Smithfield, whose prices affect meat and poultry costs throughout the UK, and Billingsgate, shifting 25,000 tonnes of fish annually, still occupy fine purpose-built Victorian buildings in east London.

Londoners are discerning food shoppers, and there's been a big revival in retail market shopping, with Leadenhall in the City and Borough Market in Southwark topping the list in terms of choice and quality. Elsewhere, street markets combine food stalls with clothes, arts and crafts and antiques. Camden is the biggest and best, but Petticoat Lane in the east, Portobello, just off trendy Notting Hill, Spitalfields, once home to Huguenot silk-weavers, and Bermondsey all have their fans, while shoppers with a real appreciation of cultural diversity head for Brick Lane.

ABOVE *London's metro system, widely known as the Tube, covers the whole capital*

BELOW *Once London's wholesale fresh produce market, the glass-roofed former Covent Garden building is now home to chic boutiques and craft stalls, and a venue for street entertainers*

LEFT *Tucked behind Covent Garden, tiny Neal's Yard is one of the best places to track down food specialities such as good breads and cheeses, or relax with a freshly ground coffee*

Buckingham Palace

Buckingham Palace, the Queen's official residence, was originally built in 1702 as the Duke of Buckingham's city house. In 1762 it was sold to George III as a private dwelling for Queen Charlotte. During the 1820s it was enlarged according to designs by John Nash, becoming the monarch's official London residence with the accession of Queen Victoria in 1837. More alterations in 1913 produced today's building, a 300-room colossus whose sumptuous state rooms are open to the public during the summer.

The palace stands at the head of the Mall, an arrow-straight, tree-lined avenue that sweeps through St James' Park, the oldest of the royal parks, down to Trafalgar Square via the grandiose Admiralty Arch. On state occasions the Mall lies on the route of all ceremonial processions, an aspect of British life that enthrals foreigners and brings a swell of pride to native 'Brits', who firmly believe – with some justification – that no other nation puts on as good a show of pageantry as the British.

The hallmarks of the big occasions are immaculate marching, brass bands, colourful army uniforms and gleaming horses. Many of these elements can be enjoyed on a daily basis at the ceremony of the Changing of the Guard outside Buckingham Palace, when a detachment of the Queen's Foot Guard marches up the Mall to replace the outgoing guard at the entrance to the Palace.

ABOVE *Serried ranks of summer planting flank the Victoria Memorial in front of Buckingham Palace. The monument was erected by Edward VII in tribute to his late mother*

LEFT *A band of guards from the Household Regiments march smartly up the centre of the Mall during a ceremonial event*

Southeast England

This corner of the country has long been under pressure from London, whose urban sprawl spreads relentlessly southwards as the demand for housing and 21st-century amenities increases. To the south and east of the capital spread the densely populated Home Counties, a swathe that extends from Hampshire to the Kent coast. Despite the pressures of population, the southeast has retained glorious countryside, historic towns and a superb coastline, all of which provide escape and recreation for the millions of people living in, or on the fringes, of the capital.

Along this coastline are sited the main Channel ports of Dover and Folkestone, Ramsgate and Deal, their history bound up with the story of threats of invasion over the centuries. Julius Caesar landed here in 55BC, William the Conqueror won England in a battle just outside Hastings in 1066, and during World War II the skies over the Weald of Kent were the scene of the Battle of Britain. The towns and cities of this region are rich in history, from Canterbury, where Christianity first took root, to Portsmouth, home to the Royal Navy, and Windsor, its castle a mighty expression of royal power.

Away from the holiday bustle of its seaside resorts, the southeast has hung on to great stretches of untouched and protected landscape. These include the great walking country of the North and South Downs, and the ancient woods and heathland of the New Forest, where, a short walk from the car parks, there's utter peace and an abundance of wildlife.

Piers, with their promenades and amusements, were an essential element of the development of English holiday resorts. Eastbourne's splendid example dates from 1872

The Sussex Coastline

ABOVE *The dazzling white cliffs of the Seven Sisters drop down to sea level at the tiny settlement of Cuckmere Haven*

OPPOSITE *The first lighthouse on Beachy Head was built in 1702. This one, at the foot of the receding cliffs, dates from 1902*

Between Seaford and Eastbourne the coastline rises to the spectacular cliffs of Beachy Head. Here, where the South Downs meet the sea, vast cliffs of pure white chalk rise vertically from the water to a height, at the headland, of 536ft/163m.

There's no beach below – the name comes from the Norman French words *beau chef*, meaning 'beautiful head', and Britain's highest chalk sea cliff is certainly that, with panoramas east to Dungeness in Kent and west into West Sussex. Its startling whiteness is due to the constant process of erosion along this stretch of coast. The sea gnawing at the base of the cliffs causes regular landfalls,

which expose new layers of clean chalk, and as a result the cliffs are receding at about 12 inches/30cm each year.

This process continues along the neighbouring cliffs of the Sussex Heritage Coast, a stretch of sharp rises and dips known as the Seven Sisters. A footpath, the start of the 80-mile (129km) long South Downs Way, runs along the top, linking the famous cliffs and providing one of the most exhilarating and impressive walks in the region. The track finally drops down into the valley of the River Cuckmere and Alfriston, a beguiling village whose 14th-century parish church is known as the Cathedral of the Downs.

RIGHT *The magnificent 16th-century Christ Church Gate, ornately decorated with symbols of the Tudor kings, gives access to the precincts of Canterbury Cathedral*

Dover

The White Cliffs of Dover, for centuries the first or last sight of England for many travellers, majestically flank one of Britain's major sea ports.

The Romans saw the defensive potential and chose this coastal point as the base for their northern fleet, building a lighthouse to guide in their ships. That lighthouse is now enclosed by the massive fortifications of Dover Castle, constructed in 1168 by the Normans and still in use as a military installation up until the 1980s.

Beneath the keep the cliffs are a warren of tunnels that were excavated during the Napoleonic wars. They found another purpose during World War II, when they were used as the planning headquarters for the evacuation of Allied troops from the beaches of Dunkirk. Today the tunnels are a major tourist attraction.

Canterbury

In medieval times Dover was the entry port for thousands of pilgrims en route to the famous shrine of the martyr St Thomas à Becket at Canterbury, some 16 miles (26km) inland to the north. It was a pilgrimage celebrated by the poet Geoffrey Chaucer in his bawdy *Canterbury Tales* of c.1390.

Historic Canterbury is still partly ringed by ancient defensive walls. Its fine cathedral, which incoporates an original Norman crypt, is the mother church of the Church of England. This was the scene, in 1170, of the murder of the Archbishop Thomas à Becket on the orders of Henry II. Near by are the scant ruins of England's first Christian complex – an abbey founded by St Augustine in 598, and England's oldest Christian site, St Martin's, where King Ethelbert was baptised in 597.

BELOW *The walls and keep of Dover Castle, high above the busy European ferry terminal, enclose a Roman pharos (lighthouse) and a 7th-century Saxon church*

Rooms
Available

Rye

An attractive mix of half-timbered and tile-hung Tudor brick cottages, imposing Georgian houses and cobbled streets, the ancient town of Rye perches on a sandstone hill above the River Rother and the expanse of the Romney Marshes.

In the middle ages Rye was an important port and a proud member of the confederation of the Cinque Ports, established by Edward I in 1268 to provide the monarch with maritime support in return for trading privileges. By the 18th century these rights were interpreted by local sailors as a licence for large-scale smuggling, viewed by the townspeople as a perfectly legitimate trade, and many of Rye's finest houses were built with the ill-gotten profits.

Today Rye's sea harbour is gone, the river is silted up and the town now lies peacefully marooned 2 miles (3km) inland. It remains a prosperous market centre, whose myriad weekend visitors come to stroll through the picturesque lanes, browse in the antique shops and take in the Ypres Tower, once used as a lookout point for cross-Channel invaders.

Rye hosts an annual Literary Festival, considered among the liveliest in England. It is a fitting event for a town which numbers writers such as Henry James and E F Benson among its former citizens.

ABOVE *Rye's windmill replaced an earlier, 16th-century version in 1932, and housed a bakery and pottery before becoming a well-known guest house*

LEFT *Sloping Mermaid Street contains some of Rye's most venerable buildings, such as the timber-framed 16th-century Old Hospital and Lamb House, once home to American novelist Henry James*

Brighton

Brash, buzzy Brighton is the southeast's major resort. It set the trend for seaside frolics back in the 1780s, when the Prince of Wales (the future George IV) took up the newly fashionable pastime of sea bathing and came to the tiny fishing village of Brighthelmstone with his mistress, Mrs Fitzherbert.

As Prince Regent after 1810, he had the money (and the authority) to build himself a pleasure palace, the extraordinary Royal Pavilion, whose flamboyant architecture earned it its own sobriquet: Oriental-Gothic. All Indian- and Chinese-inspired domes and minarets outside, the Pavilion's interior, complete with chandeliers, glittering cupolas and a vast banqueting hall, set the standard for what was to become the wonderful tackiness of the town.

Thousands of London day-trippers, liberated by the railways, poured here in the 19th century, and it was for their amusement that two splendid piers were built, one still functioning today. Modern Brighton, with its Georgian houses, and classy antique shops and smart restaurants in the warren of old streets known as the Lanes, tries hard to sell itself as a middle-class town, but the big student presence, the free-spending weekenders and Britain's most thriving gay community ensure that it will never – thankfully – quite shake off its blowsy image.

ABOVE *Brighton station acquired its ornate clock in the 19th century, when thousands of London workers came by train for a taste of the pleasures of the seaside*

LEFT *The Palace Pier was built in 1899 and remains the centre of traditional seaside amusements in Brighton, with every visitor coming to experience the Pleasure Dome, the Palace of Fun, fairground rides, candy floss, ice cream and fish and chips*

BELOW *The architect John Nash was responsible for transforming a simple Georgian farmhouse into the exuberant Royal Pavilion in 1815*

Bodiam Castle

From the time of the Norman invasion in 1066, the English aristocracy built themselves fortified castles, both as places of refuge and as grandiose statements of their power and wealth. Many still survive, and through them can be traced the evolution of castles from defensive strongholds to huge mansions designed for sybaritic living.

The southeast is rich in such castles, some virtually unchanged since medieval times, others that have been refashioned over the centuries as needs and fashion dictated. Early castles had the additional protection of a moat, and few are more impressive than Bodiam in East Sussex. It was built in 1383 as a refuge from French invaders and stands as a perfect example of a medieval castle, with towers and battlements reflected in the surrounding waters. Despite a skirmish in 1484, its defensive powers were never really tested.

BELOW *Bodiam is a late example of a French design castle, forming a perfect square around the moat, with imposing gatehouses to the front and rear*

Royal Ascot

In 1711, while riding out from Windsor, Queen Anne came across a patch of open heathland that seemed an ideal place for 'horses to gallop at full stretch'. The area was called East Cote, and by August of that year a course had been built and Royal Ascot was born. There were one or two setbacks to the growth of Ascot's popularity – George I was totally uninterested in racing – but by 1760 Ascot was established as a focal point of fashion for anyone passionate about horse racing. In 1790 George III had a temporary stand erected for himself and his guests; this was the first Royal Enclosure, accessible only by royal invitation, and today it's the area from which the royal family and thousands of patrons watch the meeting.

Every monarch since the time of George III has come racing during Ascot Week, whose pattern, since the early 20th century, follows a strict timetable. The Queen and the Duke of Edinburgh attend every day during the meeting, driving from Windsor Castle and processing down the course to the royal box in open landaus, accompanied by their guests. The Queen is a passionate horsewoman and owner, who has had 19 wins at Ascot over the years.

For many race goers, though, horses come a poor second place to fashion and fun, for Ascot, of all British race meetings, provides a glorious excuse to dress up, particularly on the Thursday of Ascot Week: Ladies' Day.

BELOW *The Queen and the Duke of Edinburgh acknowledge the crowds from their carriage on Ladies' Day, in June 2004*

OVER *Passion and enthusiasm for the 'Sport of Kings' ignite race-goers in the Silver Ring at Royal Ascot*

LEFT *Ladies' Day is the perfect opportunity to make a fashion statement; many race goers now attend as part of a corporate entertainment package*

INSIDE *Brightly coloured silks worn by the jockeys make identification easy as the field of the Jersey Stakes thunders down the course*

Knebworth

By Tudor times the building style favoured by the wealthy and powerful was changing. In Hertfordshire in 1490 the Lyttons built Knebworth, a magnificent mansion that has been substantially altered as the family's circumstances changed. In its original form Knebworth was a great Tudor courtyard house, augmented in later, Jacobean times with a superb banqueting hall, complete with screen and panelling, and a grand staircase.

The year 1811 saw the start of a massive building programme which transformed both the interior and the exterior of the house. The change was instigated by the Victorian novelist, poet and playwright Edward Bulwer-Lytton, who favoured the ornamental splendours of the high Gothic style.

In the early years of the 20th century Edwin Lutyens and Gertrude Jekyll redesigned the gardens to provide a foil for the neo-Gothic battlemented magnificence of the main building. Today Knebworth is as much a reflection of a 19th-century country house as of an Elizabethan mansion.

ABOVE LEFT *Knebworth's battlements and turrets rise above a sheltered knot garden, Jekyll's interpretation of a traditional Tudor herb and pleasure garden*

ABOVE *Knebworth, like many mansions, is adorned with heraldic beasts holding shields that bear the armorial crests of the owners*

The South Downs

The South Downs are a long ridge of chalk upland, with an escarpment to the north and a gentle sloping plateau to the south. They stretch across the counties of Sussex and Hampshire, extending from Beachy Head to Petersfield. Small villages of sandstone, flint and brick cluster at their foot on either side, but the ridges are empty – perfect walking country that gives thousands of people the chance to escape the tumult of this heavily-populated corner of England.

The 100-mile (161km) South Downs Way, Britain's first long-distance bridleway, follows the old routes and droveways of ancient people along the crest of the Downs, passing hillforts and tumuli that bear witness to the earliest downland settlers.

Lewes

North of the eastern Downs lies the town of Lewes, a Saxon foundation that retains its medieval street plan, along with many fine Georgian houses. Its history is celebrated by Bonfire Societies which, on November 5th, process through the town with flaming torches before lighting huge fires on which are burnt effigies of Guy Fawkes and the Pope. In many ways a private festival, it traditionally commemorated the execution of 17 local Protestant martyrs between 1555 and 1557. Today it's mainly about local pride and independence and is enjoyed by all members of the community.

BELOW *William de Warenne, William I's son-in-law, was gifted the town of Lewes after the Norman Conquest, and built a castle on one of two mottes, or mounds*

OPPOSITE *The rolling uplands of the South Downs above Seaford in East Sussex provide a tempting subject for artists*

Portsmouth

Britain's proud seafaring past meets its modern, streamlined naval present in the city of Portsmouth, located on the broad peninsula of Portsea Island and overlooking the world's second largest natural harbour. Henry VII established a royal dockyard here in the 15th century, and Portsmouth today combines its role as the country's most important naval base with that of a witness to the nation's seagoing past.

The town has twelve museums, many with maritime themes, and of these, it's the complex of the historic dockyard at the Royal Naval Base that attracts most visitors. Here is preserved HMS *Victory*, Admiral Lord Nelson's flagship at the Battle of Trafalgar in 1805. Nelson was fatally wounded in the battle, and the spot below decks where this great hero died is still proudly pointed out by naval guides. Other historic ships on the site include the recovered remains of the Tudor *Mary Rose*, Henry VIII's flagship, which capsized spectacularly in

1545, drowning most of the 700-strong crew before the King's eyes. The youngest vessel here, the early iron-clad warship HMS *Warrior*, dates from 1860. Visitors can learn more in the nearby Royal Naval Museum, which tells the full story of British naval history.

Elsewhere in Old Portsmouth (the original town by the harbour entrance), there are fine Georgian buildings along the High Street, site of the much-altered 12th-century cathedral. Behind here, Tudor fortifications give bird's-eye views over the ceaseless comings and goings on the waters of the Solent, which bustle with modern naval vessels, pleasure boats and the regular ferries to France and the Isle of Wight.

There are more staggering views from the enclosed viewing platform of the new Spinnaker Tower, a 540ft/165m high sleek, modern structure on Gunwharf Quay, the waterside stretch of stylish shops, bars and restaurants that represents the 21st-century city.

ABOVE *The design for the Spinnaker Tower, despite being approved by the local population, attracted controversy for its dominance of the historic harbour area*

OPPOSITE *HMS* Victory *is the only great wooden battleship to be completely preserved. She was built in 1765 and continued in service for 20 years after the Battle of Trafalgar*

LEFT *Life below deck on warships like* Victory *was extremely cramped, with sailors and gunners sleeping in hammocks (stowed during the day) right beside the cannons*

The New Forest

Nowhere else in this region does the rural present meet the past as strongly as in the New Forest, a 144-square mile (373sq km) expanse of Hampshire heath, grassland, bog and woodland requisitioned in 1079 as a royal hunting preserve by William I, and still administered by the Crown.

William enacted draconian Forest Laws to preserve the precious deer, but pressure from forest dwellers forced later monarchs to concede rights, many of which still exist. The main privileges, held by the Commoners of the Forest for the last 900 years, include the pasturing of ponies, cattle and pigs in the open forest. Today, Commoners' rights are overseen by the ancient Court of Verderers, whose role was once to enforce the Forest Law – which punished severely anyone who interfered with the deer and their food.

Together, Commoners and Crown have shaped the landscape of the forest, whose flora is defined by what the deer and domestic stock will, or will not, eat. The result is a beautiful area of woodland and open country, one of southern England's most valued playgrounds, visited by more than 8 million people annually.

The best way to enjoy it is to walk or ride over the 150 miles (240km) of tracks that weave through the area, before exploring its two loveliest villages, Beaulieu and Buckler's Hard. The latter is an Elizabethan shipyard settlement, where men o' war were once constructed from the giant oaks of the Forest.

BELOW *The tiny Sika deer have bred successfully across the New Forest since a pair escaped from Beaulieu in 1904. Their numbers are controlled at around 2,000 by annual culling*

OPPOSITE *Traditional woodland management across the New Forest has produced superb habitats for wildlife and plants*

Windsor Castle

England's premier castle (and the Queen's favourite royal residence) dates from 1080, when William I built a stronghold on the one defensible site on the Thames west of London. His motte now forms the base of the Round Tower, built by Henry II, the first of a succession of major works that transformed the castle over the centuries. Chief among these was the construction, from 1475 to 1528 in the Lower Ward, of St George's Chapel – a supreme example of Perpendicular Gothic – and the embellishment of the staterooms in the early 19th century. Today Windsor is a definitive statement of the wealth and power of the monarchy, a stunning complex of historic buildings whose interiors showcase all that's finest in architecture, art and interior decoration.

The castle's exterior appearance dates from the early 19th century, when James Wyatt remodelled the towers and battlements, and the silhouette dominates the surrounding town and extensive surrounding parkland. The interior is packed with treasures, including a superb picture collection with works by Holbein, Rubens, Van Dyck, Gainsborough and Canaletto, exquisite wood carving by Grinling Gibbons, fine porcelain and furniture. In 1992 a major fire damaged parts of the castle, and its brilliant restoration illustrates the range of specialist expertise still thriving in modern Britain.

ABOVE *Castle guards come from the seven Household Regiments, whose duties include performing ceremonial functions as well as acting as part of the modern army. The ceremony of Changing of the Guard takes place at Windsor daily*

LEFT *Windsor Castle, once an isolated stronghold, now lies less than half an hour from central London, right underneath the Heathrow flightpath*

RIGHT *Banners of the Knights of the Garter – a chivalric order whose membership is in the Queen's gift – hang beneath the delicate stone tracery of the roof of St George's Chapel*

Southwest England

Southwest England covers the area south and east of the Bristol Channel: the counties of Wiltshire, Dorset, Somerset, Devon and Cornwall. Far enough west to escape London's magnetic pull, this is a predominantly rural area, marked by serene market and cathedral towns, and embraced by some of Britain's most beautiful, and geologically most ancient, coastline.

Bristol, its one major city, lies to the north, with Plymouth to the south. Inland, the centre encompasses rolling countryside and a string of thriving towns, many with history dating back to Roman times. Earlier still, this area was home to prehistoric tribes, whose legacy is the great monuments of Stonehenge and Avebury on Salisbury Plain. To the west, the ancient Celtic race gave Cornwall its unique place names.

The southwest is rich in legend – the home of King Arthur in the 6th century. Some 300 years later the embryonic country of England emerged from Alfred's kingdom of Wessex. Alfred regrouped his forces to fend off the Danes in the heartland of the Somerset Levels, a unique lowland area that was once flooded by the sea.

West from here, the fertile red acres of Devon are slashed by two great upland areas, Exmoor and Dartmoor, providing a foretaste of the diverse grandeur of the Cornish coast. This rugged and beautiful coastline, once the world's largest tin producing region, now attracts thousands of visitors to its beaches, making Cornwall one of Britain's favourite holiday areas.

The silhouette of St Michael's Tower tops
Glastonbury Tor, Somerset, a distinctive
conical hill 521ft/158m high, where ley lines
meet at the heart of the mystic Vale of Avalon

Stonehenge

Nine miles (14km) north of Salisbury stands the ancient stone structure of Stonehenge, a UNESCO World Heritage Site and the most famous prehistoric monument in Europe.

Today's monoliths and trilithons – those pairs of upright stones crossed by a lintel – were originally part of a much larger complex, whose significance has been disputed by archeologists for many years. Theories about Stonehenge's purpose range from a role as a place of ritual sacrifice and sun worship to a giant astronomical calendar.

Construction probably took place in several stages, commencing around 3,000BC with the building of the outer banks and ditch and finishing about a thousand years later, when the last of the great sandstone sarsens was raised. The stones for this inner circle came from the neighbouring Marlborough Downs. The bluestone outer trilithons, however, were somehow transported to the site all the way from Preseli in Wales.

Despite restrictions of access among the actual stones, and the constant noise from two nearby roads, Stonehenge remains an evocative place, its atmosphere and 'vibes' drawing thousands of druids, New Age travellers and ordinary folk who come here each year to celebrate the summer solstice.

ABOVE *Sunset behind the powerful outline of Stonehenge, the mysterious monolithic stone circle on Salisbury Plain*

LEFT *Sunlight illuminates the carefully dressed stone of two 3,000-year old trilithons at Stonehenge. These 13ft/4m giants were transported from Wales*

The Dorset Coast

Dorset's coastline forms the sea fringe of one of southern England's loveliest and most rural counties; a glorious stretch of beaches, downs and cliffs that runs from Bournemouth in the east to Lyme Regis in the west. The area draws hordes of summer visitors who come to enjoy traditional seaside holidays at resorts like Swanage and Weymouth, walk the Southwest Coast Path and explore beguiling small towns such as Bridport and Lyme Regis.

Lyme, a classy little town packed with Georgian houses and fronted by the solid stone mass of the curving harbour wall known as the Cobb, has drawn fossil hunters ever since the 18th century. The geologically complex structure of the cliffs here, which are known as the Jurassic Coast, provides perfect conditions for fossil preservation, while their inherent softness causes frequent landslips that expose the fossils. In 1811 Mary Anning, a 12-year-old local girl, discovered an almost complete skeleton of a 33ft/10m ichthyosaurus, now one of the best-known exhibits in London's Natural History Museum.

East of Lyme rise huge sandstone cliffs, with Golden Cap, at 627ft/191m the highest point on the coast, providing a superb vantage point over the whole of Lyme Bay. East again, the cliffs give way to the more gently rolling green hills that back 17-mile (27km) long Chesil Beach, an extraordinary wide, 50ft/15m high storm beach

ABOVE LEFT *There's something for all the family to enjoy on the beach at Weymouth*

ABOVE RIGHT *Tumbled boulders at Mupe Bay near Lulworth Cove; the coast here is fascinating for geologists*

LEFT *The perfect curve of Lulworth Cove, east of Weymouth, was formed when the sea broke through the sandstone of the cliffs and eroded the land behind. Today it's a welcoming haven for small summer craft*

ABOVE *Like Lulworth Cove, the limestone natural arch of Durdle Door was formed by sea erosion over thousands of years*

RIGHT *A keeper at Abbotsbury Swannery takes a wild mute swan to be checked over. The first swans were introduced in medieval times by the monks of the local Benedictine abbey*

OPPOSITE *The rolling chalk of Swyre Head and Bats Head, west of Durdle Door, is stiff walking for hikers on the Southwest Coast Path*

of pebbles. Due to the action of wickedly strong coastal currents, the beach's pebbles range from fist-size at Portland in the east to 'pea gravel' at Burton Bradstock in the west.

As you continue east, Weymouth is the main resort on this stretch of the coast, a perfect base for exploring Lulworth, Caldon Down and the Purbeck Hills. These mark the entrance to the Isle of Purbeck – not really an island, but a promontory of heathland south of Poole harbour, with a distinctively insular feel. It contains the pretty village of Corfe Castle, over which rise the ruins of the castle itself, once a Royalist stronghold, which was besieged and taken by the Roundheads during the English Civil War.

Poole Harbour is a huge expanse of water, which contains wooded Brownsea Island, a haven for red squirrels and wading birds. Poole itself adjoins Bournemouth, a resort and favoured retirement town founded in 1811, with a glorious sandy beach and superb stretches of public gardens.

Bath

The city of Bath lies on either side of the River Avon in a bowl of hills, up whose slopes are stacked Georgian terraces built during the city's 18th-century heyday as England's leading spa, where fashionable society flocked to take the waters.

Centuries earlier, Bath developed as Roman Britain's top spa town, named Aquae Sulis, with a magnificent bathing complex that included the 110ft/33.5m long Great Bath. Today it is fed by the same spring, whose waters remain at a constant 46.5°C.

By 1720 Bath was once more in vogue with the leisured classes, and two architects – father and son, both named John Wood – were responsible for the city's transformation from a medieval town with a fine abbey to England's most perfect Georgian ensemble. They designed a whole new town, with classically inspired crescents, streets and circuses around the Assembly Rooms, where visitors gathered for gossip and entertainment. Later architects added the Pump Room, Pulteney Bridge and more terraces and squares.

Today Bath offers some of the best shopping, eating and cultural life in the whole of the southwest, and the future of this World Heritage city seems assured under the care of the Bath Preservation Trust.

ABOVE *Victorians across Britain benefited from mineral water drinks produced from Bath spa water*

RIGHT *Medieval Bath Abbey rises behind the Roman Great Bath, today overlooked by the windows of the Georgian Pump Room, built in 1786 for spa visitors*

TOP *John Wood designed the Royal Crescent, built between 1767 and 1775, a graceful curve high above the city that's considered one of Europe's great architectural set pieces*

ABOVE *Pulteney Bridge, designed by Robert Adam in 1769, spans the River Avon and is lined with tiny shops and flanked by an elegant arcade*

49

Exmoor

The high plateau of Exmoor rises to the south of the Bristol Channel, a national park sprawling across north Somerset and into Devon that's cut through by the wooded river valleys of the Exe, the Barle and the Lyn. Its 30-mile (48km) long coastline is both dramatic and beautiful, but it's the high interior moorlands that attract thousands of walkers, horse riders and nature lovers each year.

Exmoor has over 600 miles (960km) of footpaths and bridleways, tracks that traverse what, in bad weather, can be some of England's most forbidding landscapes. The upland heart is home to wonderfully diverse flora and fauna, including birds of prey, England's only wild population of red deer, and the unique Exmoor ponies. This stocky species, thought to be closely related to prehistoric horses, can be seen grazing the treeless wastes at the centre of the moor around Simonsbath, centre of the ancient hunting reserve known as Exmoor Forest. Simonsbath stands on the River Barle, west of postcard-

ABOVE The rugged crags of the Valley of the Rocks, near Lynton, have been attracting walkers since the poet Coleridge first hiked here from the Quantocks

OPPOSITE Dunkery Beacon, at 1705ft/519m Exmoor's highest point, affords superb views north towards Porlock, the Bristol Channel and the Welsh coast beyond

pretty Winsford, where thatched cottages surround the green. The hamlet of Exford, north of here, is the base for walkers tackling Dunkery Beacon. On the southern edge of the moor, Dulverton is home to the park authority.

Exmoor's northern edge runs along the sea to the west of Minehead, the starting point for England's longest and most spectacular long-distance footpath, the Southwest Coast Path, which runs for 630 miles (1,014km) around the southwest tip of the country. In Exmoor it passes through Porlock, a village cupped by hills and crammed with thatch-and-cob houses. It was 'a person on business from Porlock' who famously interrupted Samuel Taylor Coleridge as he scribbled down his opium-induced poem 'Kubla Khan', in 1797 – the epic work was never completed.

The best time to explore Exmoor is in summer, when the heathland is painted with spreads of gorse, ling and bell heather, and the views down to the coastal villages of Lynton and Lynmouth are at their best.

Resorts of the Southwest

BELOW *Traditional Punch and Judy shows are still part of English children's seaside holiday memories*

BELOW *Traditional Punch and Judy shows are still part of English children's seaside holiday memories*

England's southwest is seaside holiday country *par excellence*, with resorts that fit the bill for every variety of pleasure seeker.

Mass air travel to the Mediterranean lured thousands away from England in the 1970s, forcing many traditional centres to sharpen up their acts and provide alternative diversions for those inevitable English summer days when the sun doesn't shine. Weymouth is a case in point – an old port that was transformed into a booming Victorian resort, complete with Esplanade and golden sand, and which now pulls in the 21st-century trippers with its sea-oriented visitor attractions. Further west, Torquay and the surrounding Torbay area sells itself as the 'English Riviera', complete with a mini-corniche, exuberant municipal planting and rows of palms which flourish in this sheltered, sunny spot.

There's nothing sheltered about the wild north coast in the neighbouring county of Cornwall, where the pounding seas hit England's westernmost point at Land's End. The full force of the Atlantic lies behind the waves on this coast, drawing in surfers from all over the world. Their mecca is Newquay, an unashamedly brash, youth-oriented surfer's paradise centred around 7 miles (11km) of wide, sandy beaches, where the breakers rival anything available in Europe.

The resorts of Cornwall's south coast have a very different appeal. Here, flooded river valleys known as rias penetrate deep inland. They provide marvellously sheltered waters for sailing enthusiasts, who flock to the waters around Fowey, St Mawes, Falmouth (where you'll also find the Cornish branch of the National Maritime Museum) and the wide, wooded Helford River.

LEFT *Beach huts, like these at Torquay, are a quintessential part of the English beach scene for changing, sheltering and relaxing*

BELOW *High summer brings hundreds of holiday makers to Weymouth's sandy beach, backed by the imposing buildings of the Esplanade*

Gardens of the Southwest

Gardening on a grand scale started in the 18th century, when new money paid for big houses and their surrounding grounds, often scattered with classical follies and eye-catchers. Landowners not only employed designers to lay out their parks, but were also the driving force behind the first plant-hunting expeditions that, over the next 200 years, were to see thousands of exotic species taking their place in English gardens.

Stourhead, Wiltshire, is among the finest of these gardens, a magical landscape centred round an artificial lake, created by damming the River Stour. The garden was laid out in 1741 for Henry Hoare, who had returned from a European Grand Tour, his head spinning with visions of a well-ordered natural paradise, dotted with temples, grottoes, bridges and statues.

By contrast with this contrived perfection, Cornish gardens in the 18th and 19th centuries always played a dual role, acting as trial gardens for establishing the rarities collected in China, India and the Himalayas, and providing pleasure parks. South of St Austell, the Lost Gardens of Heligan, rescued from overgrown oblivion in the 1990s by Tim Smit, are still true to this, drawing thousands of non-gardening visitors while acting as a living museum of the grandest type of Victorian garden.

ABOVE *Classical temples and Gothic follies are reflected in the waters of the lake at Stourhead in autumn. The planting was conceived to accentuate the buildings on the site*

LEFT *Unearthed during the restoration of the garden at Heligan, this humorous Victorian grotesque reflects changing ideas on garden design*

Dartmoor

Dartmoor, in Devon, is southern England's largest wilderness area, a 365-square mile (913 sq km) expanse of moorland and bog where granite tors (tumbled clusters of boulders of extraordinary shapes) dominate the skyline. The central plateau is high, wild and lonely, its heathery surface pockmarked with treacherous stretches of marsh and morass and prone to wild weather and impenetrable mist – conditions that seem tailor-made for the Baskerville hound featured in Conan Doyle's famous Sherlock Holmes story, set here. Around the outer edges of the barren centre are softer, greener hills, whose river valleys contain some of this national park's most characteristic and appealing villages.

Princetown lies at the heart of the Moor – a dour, granite-built settlement famed for its high security prison, which was built to house prisoners of the Napoleonic wars. The village gives access to some of Dartmoor's most beautiful country in the shape of high moor and wooded valleys, and lies within easy reach of two of the prettiest upland villages, Widecombe-in-the-Moor and Buckland. Widecombe, whose venerable church dominates the village centre, will be forever associated with the folk ballad of Uncle Tom Cobbleigh and his band of friends on their journey to Widecombe Fair – an event that's still held in early September. Dartmeet, where the waters of the East and West Dart converge, lies between the two villages, a famous beauty spot that draws thousands of tourists.

To escape the crowds, head north towards Okehampton, where there's superb walking outside prohibited times on the high ground controlled by the Ministry of Defence, which uses this area as a firing range. It's here that the full grandeur of this remote countryside can be experienced, and there's superb walking up to the moor's two highest points, Yes Tor (2,028ft/618m) and High Willways (2,039ft/621m).

There's plenty to interest nature lovers on the tops, from the sheer beauty of the wild flowers, which include rare bog plants and wild orchids, to the great variety of birdlife, which ranges from wheeling raptors such as buzzards and kestrels to the cheery stonechats and wagtails to be seen busy in the tumbling streams.

ABOVE *This derelict powder mill near Postbridge attests to Dartmoor's once flourishing tin-mining industry*

OPPOSITE *Farmers and tin-miners used clapper bridges to negotiate Dartmoor's main rivers. This one crosses the River Dart at Postbridge*

BELOW *Herds of stocky Dartmoor ponies graze all over the moor*

NEXT PAGES *From the granite tors on Dartmoor's high tops there are superb views over the moor to the softer country below*

Clovelly

Long before the first tourists discovered the West Country, Devon and Cornwall relied on fishing, farming and mining. Cornish tin mines have long been closed, but farming still flourishes, and fishing communities still cling to the edge of the sprawling coastline.

On the north Devon coast, the picturesque village of Clovelly lost its fishing industry when the herring stocks disappeared, and today relies solely on tourism. Still privately owned, the village – all painstakingly renovated cobbled streets and flower-hung, slate-roofed cottages – tumbles down a 400ft/120m cliff to the tiny harbour, one of the few safe havens on this rocky coast. So steep are its streets that all goods are still transported on sledges which, in the 1990s, replaced traditional donkey transport.

BELOW *Precipitous cliffs rise up behind Clovelly's harbour. They offer superb walking and views out to Lundy, a tiny windswept island dominated by seabirds, seals and wild goats*

Brixham

On the other side of the county, Brixham has been an important fishing port since before William III landed here in 1688 to claim the throne of England, and still supplies fish for the London markets. It's a beguiling place, its harbour packed with fishing boats – diesel-powered today, though a few examples still exist of the beautiful three-masted Brixham trawlers, with their distinctive red sails, that were built here until the 1940s. Brixham's fishermen were courageous mariners, sailing as far as the Newfoundland banks as early as the 16th century in search of cod for the European market. Today the industry goes hand in hand with the town's role as a popular summer resort, whose pleasures centre around its beaches, itc clifftop walks and its top seafood restaurants.

ABOVE *A replica of Sir Francis Drake's ship, the* Golden Hind, *in which he circumnavigated the world, shares harbour space at Brixham with the fishing trawlers*

LEFT *Brixham stalls are the best place to sample its fresh shellfish and seafood, and Brixham crab is a renowned delicacy*

CLAWS

JELLIED EELS
COCKLES
MUSSELS
WHELKS
WINKLES
OYSTERS
PEELED PRAWN
SHELL on PRAWN

CLAWS
Try Jen
Famo
CRAB
SANDW
MADE W
ALL TYP
OF BRE

CLAWS

SHELLFISH PLATTER MENU PLUS SALADS

SEAFOOD PLATTER.... £6-95.
MOULES MARINIERE.. £5-75.
PRAWN COCKTAIL.... £3-50.
SANDWICHES.. CRAB
PRAWN
SMOKED SALMON } £2-95.

TABLES AND CHAIRS FOR CUSTOMERS ONLY

St Ives

Fishing boats still sail out from the sheltered harbour of St Ives, far to the west on Cornwall's northern coast, but the great days of the pilchard fishing industry are over and the town today is better known for its compact charm and artistic connections. It is wonderfully picturesque, with white-sand beaches, narrow streets and a jumble of lichen-clad roofs drawing thousands of summertime visitors, who come to enjoy some of the loveliest and cleanest town beaches in England.

The town, with its extraordinarily pellucid light, attracted waves of artists from the early years of the last century. Among them, in the 1940s, were Ben Nicolson and his second wife, the non-figurative sculptor Barbara Hepworth, who lived in the town from 1949 until her death in 1975. Her studio and remarkable sculpture-filled garden are now a museum, while other examples of her work are scattered around the town, including a gentle *Madonna* in the 15th-century church of St Ia.

There's more 20th-century art on display at Tate Gallery St Ives, an airy and innovative modern structure overlooking beautiful Porthmeor Beach. Drenched in sea light, the Tate displays sculpture, paintings and ceramics, among which are fine examples of the potter Bernard Leach's Japanese-inspired works, and paintings by the naïve artist and fisherman, Alfred Wallis (1855–1942).

The presence of the gallery has boosted the town's image and St Ives today, with its upmarket restaurants and commercial art galleries, is markedly more sophisticated than when Virginia Woolf described it as 'a windy, noisy, fishy, vociferous, narrow-streeted town' – although she would still recognise the constricted streets and their slate-hung cottages.

LEFT *The pristine beaches at St Ives attract surfers, bathers and families enjoying the sands and the dozens of rockpools explosed by the outgoing tides*

ABOVE *Cottages lining the narrow lanes that lead down to the harbour at St Ives were once home to local fishermen. In the 1860s as many as five million pilchards were caught in the offshore waters in a single day*

LEFT *Barbara Hepworth (1903–75) designed her garden with the placing of her sculptures amidst the greenery uppermost in her mind*

RIGHT *Designed by Evans and Shalev on the site of an old gasworks, Tate Gallery St Ives opened in 1993 to display St Ives School paintings and art against the background that inspired it*

Wales

Wales is a country set apart, a distinct cultural and geographic entity that has retained its sense of nationhood for hundreds of years, producing a tangibly different mood that's obvious to anyone passing through the Marches – that beautiful country along the border with England. Although part of the British Union since 1536, the Welsh people have always kept a firm grip on their language and traditions, making Wales as distinct in its spirit as it is in its rugged mountains, rushing rivers and sinuous coastline.

Welsh is the first language of more than a million people, most of whom live in the north, but the culture associated with the language – the music, the poetry, the love of sport – flourishes as much in the industrial towns and cities of the south as in the rural heartland.

This heartland contains no less than three great hill systems – the Brecon Beacons, the Cambrian Mountains and Snowdonia – and is surrounded on three sides by a coastline of incomparable beauty. Warmed by the Gulf Stream, the coast welcomes innumerable holiday-makers, as do the hills inland. Here, hill farming has long been the traditional way of life.

Wales' major cities, Cardiff and Swansea, once dependent on shipping, coal mining and steel, have reinvented themselves as buzzing 21st-century centres, their once derelict docklands redeveloped for leisure. More than half the population live in the major towns, but all share the same pride in the country, and understand that nostalgic melancholy known as *hiraeth*, an emotion as quintessentially Welsh as the tradition of *croeso* (welcome) that greets all visitors.

The opening of Cardiff's Millennium Centre
in 2004 reinforced Welsh national pride

Cardiff

Cardiff's major development and wealth grew from the 18th-century Industrial Revolution, when the Bute family opened up the coal fields of the Welsh valleys and built Cardiff Docks. They transformed the city into one of the world's busiest ports, attracting an ethnically diverse population, many of whom lived in the famous Tiger Bay district. Industry declined after World War II, but the city received a boost in 1955 when Cardiff was proclaimed capital of Wales. The centre was rebuilt around fine

TOP *Rugby fans demonstrate the Welsh passion for their national flag, and their love of song*

RIGHT *A statue of Wales' most famous poet, Dylan Thomas (1914–53) sits outside Swansea's Dylan Thomas Theatre*

BELOW *Street sculpture in the shape of an old anchor invokes Swansea's nautical past*

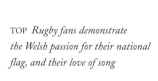

Victorian buildings such as City Hall and the Law Courts, while the university and the establishment of the Welsh Assembly in 1998 put the city firmly on the international scene. Cardiff Bay has been transformed into a superb leisure and recreational complex, and the Millennium Stadium, opened in 1999, is acknowledged as one of Britain's most exciting engineering projects.

Swansea and the Gower

Swansea, Wales' second largest city, proudly displays its industrial heriatge in its redeveloped Maritime Quarter, where 19th-century buildings house museums and Wales'

National Literature centre. Music, in the form of a major annual festival, plays a large part in the city's cultural life.

Swansea is the gateway to the beautiful Gower peninsula. The pastoral interior of this 15-mile (24km) promontory is scattered with pretty villages, while its coastline ranges from the dramatic and dangerous limestone cliffs of the south coast to the desolate sand and mud flats around Burry Inlet to the north. Its westernmost point is the Worm's Head, an impressive headland that takes its name from the Old English *orme*, meaning 'dragon'. From here, sweeping beaches, only accessible on foot, stretch north from the tiny village of Rhossili.

ABOVE *A solitary house overlooks the open sands of Rhossili Bay. The Downs, rising behind, are popular with hang gliders*

The Brecon Beacons

North of the densely populated towns of south Wales lie the Brecon Beacons, a spread of hills and valleys that was designated a national park in 1957. This beautiful area of farming country, rich in history, is scattered with small towns and villages where Welsh cultural traditions are preserved. Above it all rise the windswept mountains and open moorland.

The park covers an area of 519 square miles (1,344 sq km) and stretches from Carmarthenshire in the west through Monmouthshire, and across the English border into Herefordshire. Its hills form a quartet of upland ranges, whose central massif is the Brecon Beacons proper, high country containing Pen y Fan, at 2,901ft/886m the highest peak in south Wales, and the Beacons horseshoe, a magnificent ridge which draws thousands of walkers from the neighbouring coastal urban areas. East of here are the Black Mountains stretching from Abergavenny in the Usk valley to Crickhowell and north over the border to Hay-on-Wye. To the west of the central spurs are Forest Fawr and the high tops of the Black Mountain, a remote area with superb high-level walking along the Carmarthen Fans. Besides catering for serious walkers, the park attracts thousands who come to enjoy the fresh air, views and wildlife.

BELOW *Pen y Fan rises above the sombre waters of Llyn Cwm Llwch in the heart of the Black Mountains*

RIGHT *A powdering of snow emphasises the sparseness of the vegetation in the uplands of Waen Rydd. In summer these slopes are rich in high-altitude flora*

RIGHT *The path of the Brecon Canal, the only canal to pass almost entirely through a national park, alternates stretches of calm woodland with more exposed reaches*

OPPOSITE *The Beacons are renowned for the superb waterfalls. The Sgwd-yr-Eira falls on the River Hepste lie west of Merthyr Tydfil and the miniature Brecon mountain railway*

Llyn Safadden, the largest natural lake in south Wales, is a favourite with sailors and windsurfers.

Local towns combine a role as service centres for the surrounding hamlets and remote farms with providing accommodation and activities for visitors, and some have built a reputation on very specialised attractions. Brecon itself is one of these, an ancient riverside settlement named for a Welsh chieftan, Brychan, that stands near the site of a substantial Roman fort. Today it's a beguiling town packed with Jacobean and Georgian buildings, with a serene and austere parish church that became a cathedral in 1923. The town's modern reputation rests on the fame of its world-renowned Jazz Festival, held during August. It's also the site of the start of the Monmouth and Brecon Canal, constructed in 1797 and now partially restored.

East of here, straddling the English border at the head of what is known as the Golden Valley, Hay-on-Wye is a bibliophile's heaven. It's a tiny town, well known for its second-hand bookshops, and virtually every building is dedicated to bookselling in one way or another.

Hay's famous early-summer Festival of Literature, established in 1988, pulls in all the hottest names in the publishing world.

To the south, and easily reached from Cardiff and Newport, the pretty town of Crickhowell is packed with restaurants and gastropubs. It bills itself as the Gourmet Capital of South Wales, with restaurant menus making the most of superb local produce. North from here is Tretower Court, a stately example of an early Welsh 'gentleman's residence', complete with a 12th-century military keep and a magnificent Great Hall. The house is surrounded by a recreation of the original 15th-century garden laid out by Sir Roger Vaughan, whose family purchased Tretower in the 1420s.

South of Crickhowell lies Merthyr Tydfil. During the 19th century Merthyr became one of the world's biggest iron-producing towns, and today it draws visitors eager to explore the industrial heritage of the Welsh Valleys.

The Pembroke Coast

One of Britain's great walks skirts the whole of the Pembroke Coast in the shape of a 180-mile (288km) long path that runs from Amroth in the southeast to St Dogmael's in the northwest. It's demanding, but spectacular, walking that includes 35,000ft/10,670m of ascent and descent over its course, and takes in the most beautiful of the Welsh coastal scenery, with craggy headlands, towering cliffs, dunes and sweeping beaches.

Since 1970 this part of Wales has been a national park, whose confines stretch some miles inland and also include the offshore islands of Skomer, Skokholm, Ramsey, Grasholm and Caldey, all rich in seabirds and holding large seal colonies. To the south lie the broad sheltered waters of Milford Haven, while north rise the Preseli Hills, windswept moorland from where prehistoric man quarried the monoliths used for the construction of Stonehenge in Wiltshire.

Of the low-key settlements that hug the coast, St David's, with its cathedral dedicated to Wales' patron saint, is the most beguiling. This ancient Celtic settlement lies around Glyn Rhosyn (the Vale of the Rose), a sheltered, rising bowl containing the cathedral, which dates from the 1180s. Flooded with light, the interior has been expanded and altered over the centuries but retains a deep sense of spirituality, in marked contrast to the grandeur of the ruined Bishop's Palace, built in the 13th century and expanded to include a magnificent Great Hall by Bishop Henry de Gower in 1328.

ABOVE *Thousands of puffins visit the offshore islands to breed each year in the same burrows*

LEFT *The cathedral of St David is built on a slope, so visitors literally walk 'up' the aisle*

OPPOSITE *Point St John, near St David's, looks out towards the island of Ramsey, an RSPB reserve with large breeding colonies of kittiwakes and other seabirds*

RIGHT *Portmeirion's extraordinary buildings reflect a wide range of European architectural styles*

BELOW *Stone houses clustering around Porthmadog's sheltered harbour are roofed with the local slate*

Portmeirion and Porthmadog

Set on wooded slopes above the sheltered waters of
Traeth Bach, south of Snowdon, lies the extraordinary
Italianate village of Portmeirion. It was the brainchild
of Clough Williams-Ellis, whose life-long preoccupations
were architecture, landscape design and conservation.
He purchased the site in 1925, and by 1939 the most
distinctive buildings had been erected, though he worked
on the details until 1975. Classical façades, cupolas,
onion domes and steeples embellish the buildings, many
of which were rescued from demolition in other parts
of Britain, and this magical fantasy is surrounded by
sub-tropical gardens and miles of sandy beaches.

North from here is the harbour town of Porthmadog,
named for its founder W A Madocks, an 18th-century
entrepreneur who built a great embankment, the Cob,
across the Glaslyn estuary. This formed a natural harbour
from which thousands of tons of slate from the mines at
Blaenau Ffestiniog were shipped all over the world.

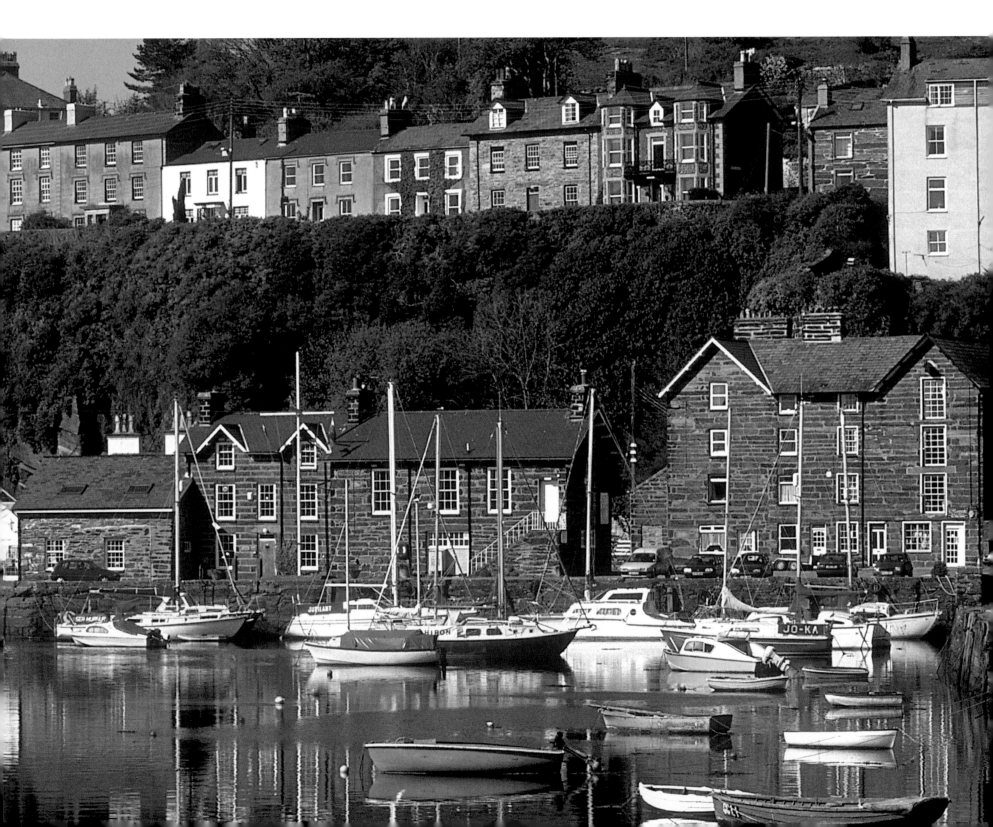

Snowdonia

North Wales is the stronghold of the Welsh language and all that signifies, and it's fitting that the region contains the iconic area of Snowdonia, home to Mount Snowdon. At 3,560ft/1,085m, Snowdon is Wales' highest mountain peak, dominating a superb swathe of dramatic upland country that slopes down to a stretch of beautiful coast. Since 1951 the area has been a national park, drawing millions of visitors, but it's also home to more than 25,000 people who live and work in its towns and villages or make their living on the hill farms.

The English gave Snowdonia its familiar name. Welsh speakers still call the region Eryri, the 'abode of the eagles', and for them it is the historic heartland of the country, forever associated with the heroes Llywelyn ap Gruffydd (d.1282) and Owain Glyndwr (c.1354–1416).

Snowdonia was one of the first of Britain's wild regions to enter the public consciousness, when late 18th-century travellers, no longer able to visit Europe because of the disruption of the Napoleonic wars, came here and found rugged landscape that rivalled anything across the Channel. Much of the ruggedness came from the great slate deposits in the hills, mined extensively in the 19th century to roof houses as far away as Australia. The slate industry was centred on the small town of Blaenau Ffestiniog.

From here the road heads north to Betws-y-Coed, a settlement beautifully placed in gentler, wooded countryside and renowned for the waterfalls in the surrounding hills. North of here, the coastline draws as many visitors as the hills, with thousands enjoying the vast beaches round Cardigan Bay. Barmouth, just north of the Mawddach estuary, is the main resort along this coast.

RIGHT *The cone-shaped summit of Tryfan rises above the Ogwen valley. The land can only support sheep, which largely live wild, only being rounded up for lambing and clipping*

Great Little Railways of Wales

BELOW *The proud feathers of
the Prince of Wales surmount
the Ffestiniog Railway's crest*

BELOW *The proud feathers of
the Prince of Wales surmount
the Ffestiniog Railway's crest*

The mountain of Snowdon rises in the north of the
region, a dauntingly wild hill that attracts thousands of
hill walkers. Even for the less fit, Snowdon's summit is
easily accessible, thanks to the Snowdon Mountain
Railway. Britain's only rack railway, it runs from the old
slate town of Llanberis up the rocky mountain slopes to
the very top of the mountain.

Feisty little trains are very much part of the Welsh
experience, with numerous small independent lines,
affectionately known as the Great Little Railways,
and the narrow-gauge Ffestiniog Railway, running the
13 miles (21km) from Porthmadog on the coast to
Blaenau Ffestiniog, takes first prize. Built in the 1830s to
transport slate from the quarries to the coast for shipment,
its wagons were originally horse-drawn, converting to
steam and carrying the first passengers in the 1860s.
Ten years later the bogie coach was invented for the
railway, and two of these carriages are still in service.

Elsewhere in Snowdonia, further narrow-gauge lines,
complete with steam locomotives, polished brass and shiny
paintwork, run through some of the park's most splendid
scenery. North of Mount Snowdon, the Llanberis Lake
Railway runs along the shores of Padarn Lake, almost
connecting with the mountain line. At Bala Lake, on
the eastern edge of the national park, a wonderfully scenic
line, dating from 1868, runs along the shore of Wales'
largest natural lake. Llangollen, to the east, has its own
railway, which chugs up the Dee valley to Glyndyfrdwy.

Further south, the Vale of Rheidol line was the last
steam railway owned by British Rail. The company
operated the 12-mile (18km) narrow gauge track that
runs inland from Aberystwyth until 1989. It was built
in 1902 to transport lead down to the coast, and the line
is among the most rugged in Britain, with spectacular
views throughout and walks to the thundering Mynach
Falls at the end of the track.

LEFT *The brightly painted
carriages of the Snowdon Mountain
Railway are dwarfed by the hills
above the Llanberis Pass as the
train approaches Snowdon's summit*

OPPOSITE *A Ffestiniog steam
engine crosses the sea embankment
on the Traeth Bach before starting
its ascent into the hills. The railway
runs year-round services along
the track*

Anglesey

To the Welsh people, Ynys Môn, the island of Anglesey, is redolent with history and culture – a treasure house of prehistoric sites and the legendary home of the Druid priesthood. It lies across the Menai Straits off the northwest coast of Wales, linked to the mainland by two bridges: a graceful suspension bridge, designed by Thomas Telford in 1826, which soars 100ft/30.5m above the water, and Stephenson's sturdier tubular span, built in 1850. From here, Telford's toll road (now the A5) arrows straight across the island to the port of Holyhead, Anglesey's largest town and the main departure point for ferries to Ireland.

Smaller by far is the village famed for having the longest place name in Britain: Llanfairpwllgwyngyll-gogerychwyrndrobwllllantysiliogogogoch, commonly abbreviated to Llanfair PG. Top of the island's most popular sites is the great castle at Beaumaris, built by Edward I to guard the Menai Straits. Plas Newydd, a magnificently sited 18th-century mansion, is known for its mural by Rex Whistler (1905–44), the largest canvas in the British Isles.

LEFT *South Stack, the far western point of Anglesey, is a dramatic headland, providing a paradise for naturalists*

ABOVE *Beaumaris, though never completed, is architecturally the most perfect of British castles. Its four successive lines of fortifications were protected by a moat and a tidal dock, which permitted ships to sail right up to the walls*

Conwy

One of the finest of Edward I's chain of castles built to subdue the unruly Welsh, Conwy is a blatant and potent symbol of royal power, built between 1283 and 1289. Its soaring curtain walls and eight massive towers rise from a rocky outcrop above the Conwy Estuary and enclose a classic two-warded interior, and a 125ft/38m long Great Hall, whose irregular shape follows the contours of the natural rock.

The drums of the towers are echoed in the design of this walled town's two historic bridges: Thomas Telford's graceful suspension bridge of 1825, and Stephenson's 1848 railway bridge, the world's first to use box girders in its construction.

Conwy also has a notable example of medieval domestic architecture. Aberconwy House was built around 1490 as a merchant's dwelling, and its timbered upper storeys contrast with the stonework of the ground floor.

Llandudno

Just 4 miles (6.4km) north of Conwy, and distinctly less warlike, lies the coastal resort of Llandudno, known as the 'Queen of the Welsh Resorts' and famed for its two beaches. The town was developed from a fishing village in the 19th century by Owen Williams, and is built on a grid plan of wide, tree-lined streets. From its spacious late-Victorian houses visitors could stroll (and still do) along the colourfully planted promenade to the elegant 2,295ft/700m pier, constructed in 1878.

From the town, Marine Drive circles the perimeter of the Great Orme, a headland to the west, up which runs a cable-hauled tramway. The Great Orme is riddled with ancient mine workings – 4,000 years ago copper from deep below the surface was traded all across Europe. A statue of the White Rabbit on the beach here celebrates Llandudno's links with *Alice's Adventures in Wonderland* author, Lewis Carroll (1832–98).

ABOVE *Britain's smallest house, just 6ft/1.8m wide and 10ft/6.1m tall, crouches below Conwy's walls*

LEFT *Llandudno is a handsome old resort set amid stunning coastal scenery*

OPPOSITE *The inner towers of Conwy Castle are surmounted by turrets to protect the Inner Ward and make it capable of independent defense*

The Vale of Llangollen

Shadowed by the Ruabon Mountains, the River Dee runs through the beautiful green Vale of Llangollen in North Wales. The valley takes its name from St Collen, a 7th-century saint who rode through here looking for a place to found his hermitage. The valley was already a holy place – Castell Dinas, above the town, was claimed as the burial site of King Arthur's Holy Grail, and the castle's 13th-century owner, Madoc ap Gruffydd Maelor, was to establish the nearby Cistercian monastery of Valle Crucis.

By 1345, Llangollen was important enough to merit a solid stone bridge, which proved a vital link during the early 19th century when Thomas Telford improved the road through here as part of the main coaching route from London to Holyhead. Telford was also responsible for the soaring 19 arches of the 127ft/38m high Pontcysyllte Aqueduct, the world's largest, which carries the Ellesmere Canal across the valley in an iron trough 1,000ft/305m long.

Better communications brought a stream of well-known visitors to the Vale, many of whom stayed with the 'Ladies of Llangollen' at Plas Newydd, an exuberantly decorated black-and-white cottage orné surrounded by Gothic gardens. Visitors still flock to Llangollen, some to fish the Dee for trout and salmon, some to walk in the surrounding hills. The vast majority come in July, when the town hosts the Llangollen International Eisteddfod, a celebration of music, poetry and culture.

ABOVE *Narrowboats are still built to fit exactly into the trough that carries the Ellesmere Canal across the Pontcysyllte Aqueduct. The canal has carried as many tourists as goods since the day it was built*

RIGHT *The ruins of 12th-century Castel Dinas overlook the Vale of Llangollen, a natural route west through the hills to Snowdonia and the coast*

BELOW *Narrowboats and their furnishings are traditionally painted with designs of castles, fruit and flowers*

Central England

Central England comprises the sweep of land, north of London, that stretches from the Welsh Marches in the west to the lonely Suffolk and Norfolk coasts in the east. Its northern boundary is Staffordshire, its main conurbation the city of Birmingham and its surrounding satellite towns.

Settled by early tribes, Romans, Saxons, Vikings and Normans, this is England's heart, densely populated but still containing areas of great beauty. The diversity of the region is immense, with landscape ranging from the rolling hills of the Cotswolds and the Malverns to the flatlands of East Anglia, and towns and villages whose architecture represents the full flowering of every English style. England's two greatest university cities, Oxford and Cambridge, lie within the region; its greatest writer, William Shakespeare, was born at Stratford-upon-Avon; and the West Midlands were the birthplace of the technological triumphs of the 19th-century Industrial Revolution.

Central England's historical wealth was mainly founded on wool, and merchant money built the great medieval houses and stately manors found throughout the region. Wool money, too, paid for glorious cathedrals such as Norwich, and dozens of fine churches, while later building was funded by the profits of industrialisation.

Turville's windmill, which featured in the classic children's film Chitty Chitty Bang Bang *(1968), perches high on a ridge above traditional cottages in this Buckinghamshire village, which was also the setting for the* Vicar of Dibley *TV series*

87

Ludlow and the Marches

ABOVE *As well as some of England's best restaurants outside London, Ludlow boasts some great pubs*

BELOW *Black and white half-timbered cottages are a keynote of Marches architecture. This row is in Dilwyn, a Herefordshire village near the agricultural town of Leominster*

Founded in 1085, when the first castle was constructed, Ludlow is a Marches town – one of a string of fortified border settlements built to keep out the Welsh. The castle was extended in the 12th and 13th centuries. By 1473 it was the seat of government for the lawless Marches and important enough to act as a royal prison, housing the boy Prince of Wales and his brother before their mysterious deaths in the Tower of London.

Ludlow town, sited on a hill above the Teme and Corve rivers, grew up around the castle, an enclosed and protected settlement surrounded by walls, well-preserved stretches of which still exist. Within this area, the original medieval street layout is lined with over five hundred listed historic buildings, many of them half-timbered. Most famous of these is the Feathers Hotel, a splendid black-and-white carved and timbered Jacobean building that's been open for business since 1619. The town today is renowned for its exceptional restaurants, its superb seasonal food markets and its drama, music and food festivals.

This area is famed for its association with A E Housman, who idealised its rural charms in his collection of lyrical poems, *A Shropshire Lad* (1896). Housman is buried in St Lawrence's Church, Ludlow. His romantic view of his native area is perfectly embodied by Stokesay Castle, north of the town, purchased by Laurence de Ludlow in the late 13th century. Ludlow added a great hall, tower and solar to the original 11th-century building, creating a picture-perfect manor house that bridges the gap between fortified and domestic architecture.

Some 20 miles (32km) northwest of Ludlow, the heath-covered ridge of the Long Mynd straddles the border. This is great walking country, and the Mynd is criss-crossed by footpaths, many of them offering sweeping views to the Black Mountains in Wales. The hikers' base of Church Stretton is a picturesque village complete with the ancient church of St Laurence, parts of which date from Norman times. From here a favourite walk leads up Carding Mill Valley, a gentle and beautiful vale from which paths lead up to the Mynd ridge.

LEFT *Geographical features in the Marches, such as the Long Mynd, form a natural boundary between England and Wales*

Liverpool

ABOVE *A statue of John Lennon stands outside the Cavern Club*

BELOW *The floodlit towers of the Liver Building, by Salthouse Dock*

The great city of Liverpool stands at the mouth of the River Mersey, still the largest port for trade with the USA's eastern seaboard. Liverpool's first docks were built in 1715, and for the next century the city was Europe's major slave port. From here, textiles, alcohol and weaponry were traded to Africa for slaves, who were shipped to the Caribbean in exchange for tobacco, cotton and sugar for the British markets. After the abolition of slavery, Liverpool's main export was people, with 9 million emigrants from all over Europe passing through on their way to the New World and Australia between 1830 and 1930. The city's own population grew five-fold as immigrants from China, the Caribbean and Ireland flooded in, making Liverpool one of Britain's earliest multi-ethnic communities, with a vibrancy that survived the late 20th-century economic downturn.

Liverpool today is experiencing a renaissance, with new jobs being created and urban regeneration high on the agenda. The dockland area, with its museums and upmarket bars and shops, is thriving, the arts scene buzzing, and a newly confident city looks forward to its role as European Capital of Culture in 2008.

The traditional pleasures are still there. Liverpool is a fine city, with two stylistically contrasting cathedrals and superb Victorian and Edwardian civic buildings that house museums devoted to everything from Liverpool life to superb collections of art. The waterside, dominated by the iconic Liver Building and the Port of Liverpool Building, has found a new role since the redevelopment of the Albert Dock. This houses no less than four museums, with one devoted to Liverpool's most famous sons, the Beatles.

Liverpool Life

Liverpool has long been one of England's most culturally diverse cities, and its Chinese community is one of the oldest-established in Europe. 'Shanghai' was the departure point for ships laden with silk and cotton, and by the 1860s Chinese immigrants were settling around the docks. The first Chinese businesses catered for the myriad seamen on the China-Liverpool run, but inter-racial marriage was not unusual and the community rapidly became an integral part of Liverpool life. The original Chinatown was demolished in the 1930s and a new area, centred on Nelson Street, developed, complete with shops, clubs and a plethora of restaurants serving some of England's most authentic Chinese cuisine.

All races are united in their passion for Liverpool's great sport, football. The city has two clubs: Liverpool, whose fans, still dreaming of the glory days of the 1970s and '80s, gather at Anfield; and Everton, a less glamorous side which nevertheless commands equal devotion at its Goodison Park grounds. Liverpool is also associated with one of Britain's most famous horse races, the Grand National, a tough race on a tough course that takes place in the spring at Aintree, just north of the city.

ABOVE *Cheering Liverpool fans lined the route as their team rode in triumph through the city after winning the UEFA Champions League in 2005*

PREVIOUS PAGES *Liverpool's Catholic Cathedral, fondly known as 'Paddy's Wigwam', was built in the 1960s; the massive bulk of the Port of Liverpool Building rises behind the restored Albert Dock; the main buildings on the waterfront are known as the Three Graces, and the most famous, the Royal Liver Building, is topped by the 'Liver Birds' – two bronze cormorants that have become the city's symbol*

LEFT *A traditional Chinese arch, among the world's largest outside Asia, marks the entrance to Liverpool's Chinatown. It was erected in 2000 to Feng Shui principles, having been built by craftsmen in Shanghai, Liverpool's sister city, and shipped to Europe*

BELOW *The bronze sculpted dragons on the Chinese Arch traditionally bring good fortune and longevity*

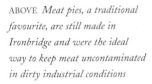

Ironbridge

Southeast of Shropshire's county town of Shrewsbury, the River Severn enters a gorge, the cradle of Britain's Industrial Revolution. It was here, in 1709, that Abraham Darby started iron-smelting using coke rather than wood, a development that enabled the invention of a process of making cast iron malleable.

His grandson, another Abraham, reaped the benefits, becoming the engineer responsible for the world's first iron bridge, a graceful 100½ft (30.6m) long single span that arches high above the Severn. It was completed in 1779, and its success did much to kick-start the giant strides in industrial manufacture throughout the West Midlands.

Up and down the gorge factories and furnaces were built, employing thousands of people engaged in smelting and the production of heavy-duty iron pieces on a scale unmatched anywhere else in the world.

By the 20th century industry had moved elsewhere and Ironbridge Gorge's importance declined. It was only towards the end of the century that it was recognised as one of the world's most important industrial historic sites and given UNESCO World Heritage status. Today the gorge's buildings house a handful of fascinating museums devoted to Britain's industrial past. Coalbrookdale iron foundry, packed with superb examples of Victorian art castings such as stags and dogs, is the best of these.

ABOVE *Meat pies, a traditional favourite, are still made in Ironbridge and were the ideal way to keep meat uncontaminated in dirty industrial conditions*

RIGHT *Fearing that it might collapse into the River Severn, Darby strengthened his 384-tonne bridge with extra struts and arches, achieving a design that made the bridge an instant sightseeing attraction*

Oxford

Synonymous with dreaming spires and gilded youth, Oxford is home to one of the world's greatest universities, whose architecturally magnificent colleges dominate the city centre. As early as the 12th century, rich bishops founded colleges, each a self-contained entity whose chapels, libraries, halls and student accommodation were arranged round a central quadrangle. Today there are 35 colleges, mainly grouped around the ancient High Street, and each with its own character and traditions.

It's perhaps the older foundations that are the most evocative, including 14th-century New College, whose buildings were the template for every collegiate design thereafter, and the sublime 15th-century complex of Magdalen, complete with Gothic cloister and its own deer park. In contrast to the restraint of these earlier foundations, grandiose structures by some of England's finest architects, such as James Gibbs' Radcliffe Camera (1737–48), Wren's Sheldonian Theatre (1663), Hawksmoor's Clarendon Building (1712) and the Bodleian Library provide an emphatic pointer to the historic wealth of the University.

ABOVE *Christchurch College was founded by Cardinal Wolsey, and its building styles vary from Tudor to 18th-century classical*

RIGHT *The Encaenia Procession en route to the Sheldonian Theatre in June. The Encaenia ceremony awards honorary degrees to distinguished men and women, and dates in its present form from 1760*

OPPOSITE *All Souls' College was founded in 1414 to commemorate those killed in the 100 Years War. Its pinnacled North Quad was designed by Hawksmoor in 1716*

94

The Cotswolds

Spreading a hundred miles through Gloucestershire and Wiltshire, the limestone Cotswolds are uplands, or 'wolds', originally full of 'cots', or sheep enclosures. England's medieval wool trade brought wealth to the area, and it was the merchants and sheep farmers who first used the glorious honey-coloured local stone to build their towns, villages, churches and manor houses. This widespread use of a homogenous building material is the key to the region's appeal, a charm that lures thousands of visitors to its timeless settlements, windy ridges and gentle valleys.

There are few large towns in the Cotswolds. Cirencester, an important Roman centre, is the 'capital', a delightful mélange of handsome buildings centred around the Market Place and dominated by the 15th-century parish church of St John the Baptist. Other Cotswold centres include Chipping Campden, a perfectly preserved medieval wool town complete with a fine church, market hall and almshouses; bustling Chipping Norton; Burford, whose glorious High Street slopes down to the River Windrush; and Moreton-in-Marsh, a buzzing market town.

But it's the villages that steal the show, a string of idyllic small settlements largely untouched by the modern development and crowds of the towns. They have names such as Bibury, Broadway, Bourton-on-the-Water, Upper and Lower Slaughter, Widbrook, Swinbrook, Great Tew and North Leach, and all feature mullion-windowed

ABOVE *A grateful nation funded the construction of the magnificent baroque Blenheim Palace, Oxfordshire, after the Duke of Marlborough's victory over the French in 1704. It was designed by John Vanbrugh and Nicholas Hawksmoor, and the landscaped park was laid out by Capability Brown in the 1760s*

RIGHT *Chipping Campden is a quintessential example of a rich wool merchants' town, packed with early Renaissance houses. Its preservation owes much to the Campden Trust, formed in 1929*

97

OPPOSITE *The 100-mile (160km) long Cotswold Way stretches along a ridge westwards from Chipping Campden almost to Bath and offers superb walking and lovely views. Turf-topped Painswick Beacon stands at the convergence of five valleys, the panorama stretching south towards Stroud*

ABOVE *Livestock husbandry still plays an important role in Cotswold life, and is celebrated at agricultural shows, like this one at Moreton-in-Marsh, throughout the summer*

RIGHT *This plaque in Kelmscot commemorates William Morris, the immensely influential writer and craftsman, who spent summers in the village from 1871 to 1896*

cottages with undulating roofs, prosperous farms and splendid churches, a dream of England that inspired the 19th-century Arts and Crafts movement. This was led by William Morris from his base at Kelmscott Manor, a house dating back to the 16th century and decorated and furnished with Morris's own designs and those of his talented friends, Edward Burne-Jones and William de Morgan.

Wool money paid for all this, and the Cotswolds today are still well-heeled. Tucked in the valleys are numerous great manor houses such as Chastleton House, Sudely Castle and Snowshill Manor. The wonderfully eccentric Sezincote is an early 19th-century confection inspired by Indian Moghul architecture, while Blenheim Palace, on the eastern fringes of the Cotswolds, remains a powerful statement of the wealth and position of the Dukes of Marlborough.

Shakespeare Country

ABOVE *Shakespeare's wife Anne Hathaway grew up at this cottage, situated on the fringes of woodland that inspired the Forest of Arden. The garden is planted with trees, shrubs and plants mentioned in Shakespeare's plays*

OPPOSITE *The River Avon flows through the middle of Stratford, a leafy waterway popular with narrowboat owners and rowers alike*

Stratford-upon-Avon is a magnet for thousands of visitors annually, who flock here to honour the memory of playwright and poet William Shakespeare, born in the town in 1564.

Without the benefit of the Shakespeare connection, the town would be an unassumingly pleasant market centre standing on the banks of the River Avon, and blessed with a clutch of attractive 16th- and 17th-century buildings. Among them is Harvard House, an ornate high street residence built by the grandfather of John Harvard, the founder of Harvard University, Massachusetts. Other houses in the town centre are associated with the great playwright, and it's these that most visitors come to see. The presence of the Royal Shakespeare Company, housed in two modern riverside theatres, ensures Stratford's pre-eminence on the provincial cultural scene.

William Shakespeare, the son of a glove-maker and a farmer's daughter from Wilcote, was born in a half-timbered house set back from the river. In 1582 he married Anne Hathaway, who was brought up at nearby Shottery. He left her, and his children, for the bright lights of London, returning to Stratford in 1597, when he purchased a house known as New Place. He died here in 1610, leaving his daughter Susanna comfortably ensconced at nearby Hall's Croft. All these buildings, and their surrounding gardens, are now Shakespeare shrines. Another is the town's handsome Church of the Holy Trinity, whose register records the playwright's death, and whose chancel holds his remains. His gravestone is inscribed: 'Good frend for Jesus sake forbeare/To digg the dust enclosed heare/Bleste be ye man yt spares thes stones/And curst be he yt moves my bones'.

Cambridge

The compact university city of Cambridge stands on the southern edge of the East Anglian fens, a golden backwater of majestic college buildings and narrow streets, embraced by the curving River Cam and the famous college Backs.

The town is ancient indeed. The original Iron Age settlement gave way to a strategically important Roman town, later developed by Saxons and Normans. The University was founded in 1209, when the first scholars fled here from Oxford, and the colleges were largely established between the 14th and 16th centuries. They usually consist of a hall, chapel, library and student accommodation grouped round a central courtyard, approached through an often magnificent gatehouse.

These front the main streets of the town, but the colleges are seen at their best from the Backs, a swathe of green land beside the River Cam, and synonymous with idyllic punting afternoons.

The university has educated outstanding writers, philosophers and statesmen. Trinity's alumni include Byron, Tennyson, William Thackeray and Bertrand Russell, as well as a trio of royals, including Prince Charles, and the Cambridge spies Blunt, Burgess and Philby. It's the biggest college, with the largest courtyard, but the architectural prize goes to the sublime ensemble of King's College. Founded by Henry IV in 1441, its lofty, fan-vaulted chapel is one of Europe's greatest Gothic buildings.

BELOW *Summer brings out the punts on the River Cam. This quintessential Cambridge activity is harder than it looks, and keeping a straight line is a real challenge*

OPPOSITE *The soaring fan vaulting and sumptuous stained glass of King's College are the backdrop for performances by the famous chapel choir, whose Christmas carol service is broadcast worldwide*

Wool Towns of East Anglia

Suffolk and Essex retain hidden corners that have been largely by-passed by modern times. They reveal beautifully preserved small market towns whose medieval wealth owes much to wool, such as Lavenham, or more esoteric luxuries like saffron, whose cultivation gave Saffron Waldon its name. Highly valued for its medicinal properties, as a dye and for culinary purposes, the saffron crocus was grown on a huge scale, surrounding the town with sheets of pale purple during the flowering season.

Wool and saffron merchants, often self-made men, used their wealth to build, erecting splendid half-timbered houses and glorious light-drenched churches. Anxious to steal a march on the less well-to-do, the most prosperous men decorated the plaster work of their houses with lavish pargetting, a process where the lime plaster within the timber frame is incised or moulded. Pargetting can be simple and low key, or immensely elaborate, with patterns changing from town to town and county to county.

ABOVE *Little Hall, built in the 15th century, stands surrounded by other timber-framed houses on Lavenham's spacious triangular Market Place*

Craftsmen worked the plaster as it dried, using stippling, dragging and combing techniques or stamping designs and raising borders using special moulds and wooden blocks. Grander buildings were decorated with swags, cartouches and friezes, borrowing designs from France, Italy and the Low Countries. The custom survives, and modern houses are still pargetted throughout these eastern counties.

Towns rich in timber-framed, thatched houses include Long Melford, Suffolk, which gets its name from its lengthy main street. Lined with splendid houses, this ends with a flourish at a wide, sloping green, where the solid stone and flint bulk of the church of Holy Trinity stands guard over a row of 16th-century almshouses.

Further down the Stour Valley the market town of Sudbury made its money through silk-weaving. It's more famous as the birthplace of Thomas Gainsborough (1727–88), England's leading 18th-century portraitist.

LEFT *The pargetting on this house in Saffron Waldon features figures and horses, perhaps a reference to the trade of the original builder*

RIGHT *The pargetting on the Old Sun Inn, Saffron Waldon, once used by Oliver Cromwell as his headquarters, is among the finest and most ambitious in Essex*

BELOW *Simpler timbered homes in Saffron Waldon use colour-wash as decoration*

Norwich and the Norfolk Broads

Sections of medieval walls still surround the heart of Norwich, Suffolk's county town, where ancient churches jostle with merchants' houses whose architecture ranges from timber-framed late medieval to serene Georgian. Dominating the narrow lanes that thread through the town are two buildings: the creamy stone bulk of the Norman castle, and the slender spire of the cathedral, founded and first built by the Normans and embellished with decorative stonework and woodcarving over the centuries.

This beautiful city was home to the artist John Crome (1768–1821), whose paintings were inspired by the Norfolk Broads, a shifting, watery landscape to the northeast. The Broads are England's largest wetland, covering 220 square miles (570 sq km), and were formed in the Middle Ages when sea levels rose. Dykes and wind pumps once controlled the waters. Today they are managed by the Broads Authority, which must balance the need to preserve the ecology of this unique eco-system with the role of the Broads as a prime recreational area.

Summer sees the rivers and lakes of the Broads packed with sailing boats and launches, but there are still vast stretches of marsh and reed where nature comes first. Hickling Broad and Horsey Mere are just two of the wildlife preserves where otters swim, bitterns boom and visitors may be lucky enough the spot the meandering flight of the swallowtail butterfly.

ABOVE *Bishop Herbert de Losing built Norwich Cathedral in about 1100. Its 315ft/96m spire was added by Bishop Goldwell after a fire in 1463 destroyed the original*

BELOW *Norwich is home to the colourful stalls of England's largest open-air market, its Market Place surrounded by civic buildings and backed by the mass of the Norman castle*

ABOVE *Wind pumps help control the levels of the waterways on the Norfolk Broads*

LEFT *Horning is one of the prime sailing centres on the Broads, and scene of the annual Three Rivers Race in early summer*

North Norfolk

The coastal lands of North Norfolk stretch beneath huge skies, a patchwork of vast beaches, shingle spits, salt marshes and dunes, backed by tranquil countryside that boasts a clutch of England's finest country houses.

These elements combine at Holkham, the home of the Coke family and Earls of Leicester, a superb Palladian mansion built by Thomas Coke between 1734 and 1761 to house the art collection he had amassed during a European tour. The Holkham estate stretches down to the sea and the village of Wells, centred round a green lined with elegant Georgian houses. Wells is one of the few places along this northern coast with a sheltered harbour, and was once a major port.

East of Wells lies Hunstanton, a settlement dating back to the 11th-century Domesday survey. The little town was transformed in the 19th century by the coming of the railway, and grew into a decorous seaside resort that still attracts the prosperous middle classes today.

A few miles south, at Heacham, the land is transformed every July into a sea of blue when the acres of lavender surrounding the village bloom. The Norfolk lavender industry was started in the early 1930s by local nurseryman Linn Chilvers. Among the many products of this thriving industry is an intense lavender perfume first made for George IV, whose formula still remains a closely guarded secret.

ABOVE *Lavender fields spread around the village of Heacham. The industry still provides jobs for local people*

LEFT *The beach at Holkham Bay,*
backed by dunes and pines, is the
largest and loveliest along this coast
and a haven for wading birds

Northern England

North of the industrial Midlands, England's landscape is transformed. Gone are the soft green fields and gentle hills of the south, giving way to a wilder, higher country, whose people are proudly and distinctly different. The northern counties of Lancashire, Yorkshire, Cumbria, Durham and Northumberland contain some of England's biggest cities, the crucible in which burned the white-hot fires of the 19th-century Industrial Revolution. Manchester, Leeds, Sheffield and Newcastle upon Tyne may have redefined themselves for the 21st century, but they remain huge urban conglomerations, in which around half England's population lives and works.

These urban centres are balanced by some of England's most beautiful countryside, a glorious mix of hills, valleys, lakes, rivers and coastal splendour, which provide both an escape for the city dwellers and a livelihood for those who still farm and fish. As early as the 1950s, much of the land came under the protection of the National Parks scheme, ensuring it would remain unspoilt, with its way of life and traditional villages and buildings protected – some would say overly so. The northern parks include the Peak District, both the Dales and northern moors of Yorkshire, and the Lake District (the most visited rural area in England). Further north in unspoilt Northumberland, castles and holy places bear witness to the region's historically rich past, on the border with Scotland.

Following his visit to the north in AD122, the Emperor Hadrian built a 75-mile (120km) long defensive wall from the Tyne to the Solway Firth to mark the northern British border of the Roman Empire. Today, its intact stretches attract thousands of walkers and sightseers to Northumberland

The Peak District

ABOVE *A Victorian pillar box at Buxton, an elegant spa town on the edge of the Peak District famed for its summer arts festival*

RIGHT *Flaky almond-flavoured Bakewell Pudding, on sale in the town, was invented by chance in 1860, when a cook's strawberry tart went wrong*

OPPOSITE *Grey stone farmhouses throughout the Peak are home to families whose living has been dependent for centuries on the price of wool*

Half the population of England lives within a day trip's distance of the Peak District, that enclave of moor and dale at the southern tip of the Pennine hills that provides the link between the harsh northern uplands and the softer green south. Since 1951, the 555 square miles (1,438 sq km) that comprise its two sections – the limestone White Peak to the south, and the northern millstone grit Dark Peak – have been a national park, providing a precious oasis of unspoilt countryside in the heavily populated and industrialised north.

The high, dry plateaux of the Peak District have been inhabited since earliest times, and almost every hilltop has a Bronze Age burial mound or barrow (known locally as 'lows'), while stone circles such as the Nine Ladies at Stanton Moor bear witness to the religious rites of ancient civilisations. As the Romans moved north in the second century, the native people retreated to the high tops, building hill forts like those above the Hope valley at Mam Tor, and leaving the invaders to exploit the

Peak's mineral wealth, mining the lead that was to remain a major source of revenue in the area right through to the 19th century.

Throughout the Peak District small towns and villages that once depended on mining and agriculture today serve the park's visitors. One such is Bakewell, an old town on the River Wye, where narrow streets and stone cottages contrast with the Georgian splendour of Bath Square – the sole remnant of an attempt to develop the town as a fashionable spa in the 18th century. East of here, Buxton thrived on the reputation of its springs, and its elegant crescents and grandiose buildings are the backdrop for a renowned arts and music festival each July.

Ten miles (16km) to the north, the pretty village of Castleton, ringed by hills and rich in sturdy cottages, draws serious walkers to the routes that fan out from here – it's estimated that over 25,000 people tackle the trails up to Mam Tor (1,696ft/517m), the second highest peak in the park. Other visitors head underground to explore

ABOVE *The River Dove sparkles through Dovedale to the north of Ashbourne in the White Peak. The walk down its gorge is one of the most popular in the national park*

RIGHT *Limestone outcrops, rich with rare wild flowers, overlook the River Manifold and its valley to the north of Ashbourne*

the limestone cave systems around the town, one of which, Speedwell Cavern, lies 600ft/183m below the surface.

Mining, quarrying and wool production filled the coffers of the Peak's great landowner, the Duke of Devonshire, who erected the great house of Chatsworth near Bakewell. Chatsworth was built on the site of a former Elizabethan manor as a grand classical house between 1687 and 1707 by William Cavendish, the 1st Duke. Packed with exceptional paintings and furniture, Chatsworth's State Rooms spread in splendour along the whole length of the south front, which overlooks the formal gardens and the vast park.

There are lower-key architectural pleasures at Haddon Hall, a mellow grey stone medieval house to the south that was sensitively restored in the 1930s by the Peak's other great lord, the Duke of Rutland.

For the majority of serious lovers of the Peak District, it's the outdoor opportunities that are the main draw. There are around 3,000 footpaths to explore. Some tracks head for the barren, peat-covered moorland of the Dark Peak, while others wend their way through the neat fields and scattered farms of the White Peak.

BELOW *Wooded parkland, designed in the 1750s by Capability Brown, surrounds Chatsworth House, country seat of the Dukes of Devonshire*

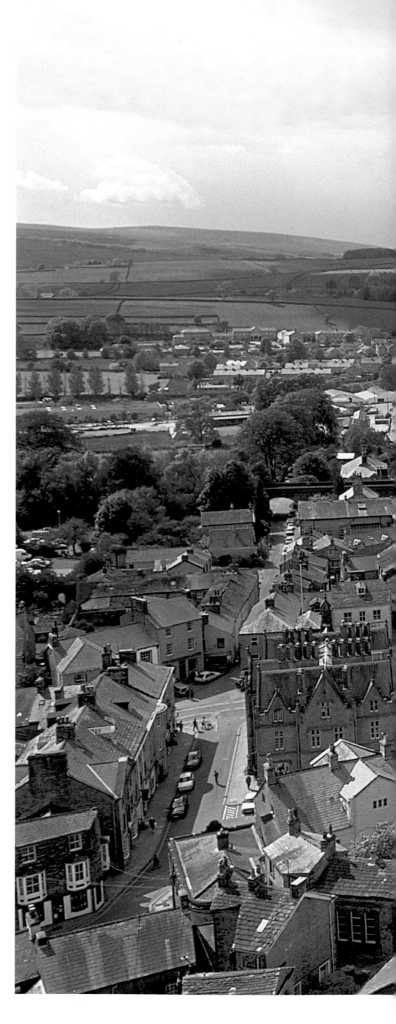

The Yorkshire Dales

East of the backbone of the Pennine hills, the Yorkshire Dales are a series of valleys running from west to east. They form a varied landscape of high limestone hills and pastoral valleys, characterised by dry stone walls and stone barns, traditionally used for storing hay and housing cattle. Like much of England's finest countryside, the area is protected by its national park status, and is rich in opportunities for outdoor activities of all kinds.

Most of the Dales take their names from the rivers that run through them, starting with Swaledale and Wensleydale in the north and spreading south to Wharfedale, Ribblesdale and Malhamdale. These three are easily reached from the market town of Settle, the terminus for the Settle-to-Carlisle railway, a 72-mile (115km) long line that's justly promoted as England's most scenic railway.

Swaledale is rich in settlements with Norse names – such as Thwaite, Keld and Muker – and the Vikings have left their legacy too, in the traditional laithes, or ancient field barns that still dot the pasture today. Found all over the Dales, they are particularly numerous here.

Swaledale is approached from the east through Richmond, a gem of a town on the River Swale. Richmond is overshadowed by the massive walls and keep of a Norman castle, high on a rocky promontory,

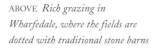

ABOVE *Rich grazing in Wharfedale, where the fields are dotted with traditional stone barns*

RIGHT *Viewed from Castleberg hill, the little town of Settle has grown up around a venerable square, which still contains the split-level, arcaded former butchers' shops of the Shambles*

ABOVE *Kilnsey Crag, Wharfedale, attracts climbers challenged by its glacially carved overhang. At its foot the still waters of a trout farm provide gentler amusement*

in which is preserved Scolland's Hall, the most ancient great hall in England. Elsewhere in the town the accent is Georgian, with attractive old buildings lining the streets that fan out from the cobbled market square. The little Georgian theatre dates from 1788, and is the oldest in the country.

To the south, Malhamdale is classic limestone countryside, dominated by the massive vertical cliffs of Malham Cove. This remarkable feature was created during the Ice Age, and is topped by a limestone pavement that's famous for its rare flora. The pretty village of Malham lies on the Pennine Way, a 256-mile (410km) trail that runs from the Scottish Borders right down into Derbyshire. In Yorkshire, it takes in dramatic landscapes that include Pen-y-Ghent, one of the hills included in the notorious Three Peaks Challenge, a 25-mile (40km), 5,000ft/1,524m combination of walking and climbing.

Ingleborough, another of the Three Peaks and easily identified by its flat top, lies to the west and overshadows the entrance to the impressive White Scar Caves. This 200,000-year-old cave system includes Battlefield Cavern, 330ft/101m long and 100ft/30.5m high, and an underground waterfall.

There's more thundering water after rain at Hardraw Force, England's highest waterfall, which is located near the Dales' main hiking centre, the market town of Hawes.

From here it's a short hop to the heart of the largest and most serene of all the dales: Wensleydale, famous for its crumbly white cheese, first made here in medieval times by Cistercian monks. The village of Wensley, attractively set round a tiny square, boasts the Dales' best church, Holy Trinity, which dates back to the 13th century. Its main rival in the area is St Andrew's at Aysgarth, a village renowned for its picturesque twin falls of water cascading over a series of broad limestone platforms.

RIGHT *The Dales are rich in limestone cliffs and turbulent rivers as here, where the River Swale drops suddenly at Wainwath Falls*

BELOW *Wharfedale scenery varies from low-lying, picture-perfect meadows to impressive limestone crags in its upper reaches*

RIGHT *The city's early history is told in a modern window in York's medieval Guildhall, reconstructed after bombing in 1942*

RIGHT *York's Town Crier still proclaims events of national and local importance, in a post that dates back to medieval times*

OPPOSITE *The Gothic-pinnacled towers of the Minster loom at one end of the ancient street of Petergate*

York

York's long history dates back to Roman times, when it was the northern capital of Eboracum, but its modern name derives from its 9th-century Danish name, Jorvik. The city was capital of the Danelaw, and the Viking legacy is still evident in its street names and the treasures in its museums. The Danes were driven out in 1066, and York's real glories, including its superb city walls, date from medieval times.

Chief among these is the Minster, England's largest cathedral and seat of the Archbishop of York. It was constructed over a period of 250 years from 1260. The immense nave is lit by windows containing some of England's best medieval stained glass, notably in the majestic East Window.

South of the Minster the cramped, narrow streets of the Shambles, lined with timber-framed houses, perfectly epitomise the medieval city, while scattered throughout old York are a further 18 medieval churches. The pleasures of modern York include a vibrant cultural scene and the lure of the famous racecourse.

North York Moors

Running from the Hambleton and Cleveland hills in the west to the dramatic cliffs of the coast in the east, the North York Moors are flat-topped, heather-clad expanses cut by deep green valleys. The area has been inhabited ever since Neolithic times, though some of its ancient forests have been replaced by modern plantations. Successive waves of settlers have left their mark in the shape of barrows and hill forts, Roman remains and the ruins of the great monastic foundations that flourished here in medieval times.

Now mainly enclosed within the borders of a national park, the moors offer splendid walking with endless views, couthy market towns and some of northern England's prettiest villages. To the west, and accessible from Thirsk and the old cobbled town of Helmsley, rise the western

moors, separated from the vale by the steep incline of Sutton Bank. These highlands are crowned by the 110-mile (176km) Cleveland Way, a long-distance path that runs across the moors and down to the coast, taking in both upland landscape and some outstanding high-cliff scenery.

Helmsley lies close to the substantial and beautiful ruins of the Cistercian Rievaulx Abbey, once the area's major landowner. The Rievaulx Terraces were built in the spirit of 18th century Romanticism to enhance the abbey views.

North of here, the wild heights of the central North Yorkshire moors rise up – superb country scattered with ancient crosses and standing stones. The loveliest village in the area is Hutton-le-Hole, a picturesque settlement

BELOW *High above Whitby harbour stand the ruins of the abbey, a great medieval centre of learning where, in 664, the Synod of Whitby decided the method for calculating the date of Easter*

LEFT *The picturesque village of Robin Hood's Bay is embraced by the curve of the cliffs. Once a thriving fishing and smuggling centre, its name has only legendary links with the outlaw hero of Sherwood Forest*

whose village green, dissected by a stream, is dotted with grazing sheep. It's close to beautiful Rosedale, site of a ruined 12th-century abbey, and Farndale, famed for its daffodils. In spring, thousands come to walk through the vast spreads of wild daffodils that grow along the banks of the River Dove at Low Mill.

The appealing old market town of Pickering is the starting point for exploring the eastern moors. It is also the home of the volunteer-run, preserved North Yorkshire Moors Railway – one of its steam engines starred as the *Hogwarts Express* in the recent Harry Potter films. The line runs to Grosmont, a village in the leafy Esk Valley, whose river runs into the sea at Whitby.

Between Whitby and Pickering stretches Dalby Forest, an expanse of moorland and conifer plantations. Its bleakness is redeemed by the charms of Thornton-le-Dale, one of the prettiest villages in the area, revealing a mixture of cottages and Georgian houses, and with an old rustic bridge at its heart.

The North Yorkshire Coast

Whitby is a gem, a bustling fishing port and resort, forever associated with Bram Stoker's gothic novel *Dracula* (1897). The town was a major centre of learning in the early Christian period, its abbey hosting the seminally important Synod of Whitby in 664. In 1746 the great mariner, James Cook, arrived in Whitby to serve his apprenticeship, and it was here that all four of his ships of exploration were eventually built: *Endeavour*, *Resolution*, *Adventure* and *Discovery*.

Cobbled Church Street is lined with shops selling the local jet jewellery, whose manufacture was once a major local industry. From its seaward end 199 steps climb up to the hilltop Church of St Mary, founded in the 12th century, giving great views over the harbour below.

From Whitby, the Cleveland Way runs north along the coast to the fishing village of Staithes, a huddle of stone houses around a harbour protected from the wild northerly winds by the towering outcrop of Cowbar Nab.

BELOW *The North York moors have numerous tree plantations like this one at Cawthorne Banks, on the edge of Cropton Forest*

OPPOSITE *Rough paths in wild upland country draw thousands of well equipped walkers to the moors*

The Northumberland Coast

ABOVE *Bamburgh Castle, built on a basalt outcrop, was an important Anglo-Saxon stronghold*

PAGE 127 *The monastery on the Holy Island, where the Lindisfarne Gospels were illuminated, was founded in 634. The castle was built in the 16th century as protection against the Scots, and remodelled by Edwin Lutyens in the early 20th century*

Peaceful under the summer sun but wild and treacherous in winter, the Northumberland coast stretches north from Newcastle to the Scottish border. This is Percy country, and two great strongholds bear witness to the power of this northern dukedom. The Percys built the mighty castle at Warkworth in the 14th century, living there for 200 years until moving to their other castle at Alnwick, an imposing pile on the edge of a bustling market town. Remodelled over the centuries, Alnwick pulls in the crowds on the Harry Potter trail – it starred as Hogwarts School in the films – and horticulturalists drawn to the computerised cascades and fountains of Alnwick Gardens, still at the

development stage. North from here, tiny villages like Craster, famed for its kippers, Embleton and Beadnell overlook huge, empty beaches, and there's windy walking out to the ruins of 14th-century Dunstanburgh Castle.

Seahouses is the departure point for the Farne Islands, a rocky archipelago that's home to grey seals and migrating seabirds. Further north, Bamburgh Castle, magnificently set above sweeping sands and rolling surf, was once capital of Northumberland; its present appearance dates from a Edwardian makeover. Huge beaches stretch up the coast, encircling the holy island of Lindisfarne, reached at low tide across a causeway.

Newcastle upon Tyne

The city of Newcastle burgeoned in the 17th century, when coal export provided the wealth for the development of shipbuilding. Two hundred years later Newcastle was building 25 percent of the world's ships. Fine civic buildings went up in the Victorian heart of Grainger Town, and the High Level Bridge was constructed over the Tyne, one of seven city bridges today.

Industrial decline hit in the 1930s and Newcastle became increasingly run down, though its warm-hearted citizens, known as Geordies, remained staunchly loyal and proud of their home. Vindication came in the 1990s, and recent years have seen an extraordinary turnabout, with Newcastle today noted as a vibrant cultural centre with a buzzing night scene. This renaissance is epitomized by the waterfront areas. To the north, the 16th-century merchants' houses of Quayside contrast with the sleek regeneration of the area beyond the Tyne Bridge – a parade of riverside promenades, squares, apartment buildings, bars and restaurants. Across the river, the Gateshead Quays are home to the BALTIC centre, a converted flour mill that's now the north's premier art factory, and the Sage Gateshead, a state-of-the-art concert venue.

BELOW *The sinuous steel and glass silhouette of Norman Foster's Sage Centre, opened in 2005*

OVER *Symptomatic of Newcastle's enthusiasm for the contemporary arts scene, thousands of people gather on the Millennium Bridge to participate in one of New York artist Spencer Tunick's naked installations*

LEFT *Antony Gormley's iconic iron sculpture,* The Angel of the North *(1998), dominates the southern approaches to Newcastle and Gateshead*

INSIDE *Sunset over the Tyne, with the looming Tyne Bridge (1928) in the background and the graceful arch of the Millenium Bridge, the world's first tilting span, in front. The bridge is designed to pivot to allow passage for ships, and is dubbed the Blinking Eye by locals*

The Lake District

Tucked within an area measuring a mere 30 miles (48km)
across lie 16 major lakes, ringed with hills and surrounded
by green valleys set with stone-built villages. This the
Lake District, England's most dramatic scenic area,
whose heart is Scafell, a volcanic dome. Around this
radiate the main lakes, all formed after the last Ice Age
as meltwater was dammed by terminal moraine. Early
inhabitants cleared the high forests, a process continued
by the Romans who left land fit to farm for the Vikings,
evidence of whose occupation is echoed in the area's
place names.

Discovering Lakeland

For centuries this was regarded as remote, hard country,
its scenic grandeur viewed with awe by all but its own
people. Attitudes changed at the end of the 18th century
with the start of the Romantic Movement, which bought
painters and poets such as John Constable and William
Wordsworth to the area. Blown away by its splendour,
they celebrated its landscape in art and writing and
attracted the high-spending visitors who could no longer
indulge in Grand Tours on a European mainland torn by
the Napoleonic wars. It was the start of the British love

ABOVE *One of the loveliest of the lakes, island-studded Derwentwater has excellent walking at lake level or along the ridge of Cat Bells to the west. Launches cruise the lake from Keswick, a busy market and tourist town on the lake's north shore*

LEFT *Herdwick sheep in Eskdale. Toughest of all British breeds, they were introduced to the Lake District by the Normans for their hardiness and wool, which is still used for carpet-making*

129

ABOVE *Shops in the market town of Kendal cater as much for visitors as for the local farming community*

RIGHT *A 4-mile (6.4km) lake-level path circles Buttermere, while there's a classic, more demanding, circuit along the ridge of Red Pike, seen here on the far side of the lake*

affair with the great outdoors – an affair that over the last two hundred years has brought town dwellers not only to the Lakes, but also to every other wild corner of the British Isles.

The Lakes Today

The Lake District today is a national park, attracting millions of visitors annually, who come to relax around the lakes and potter in the villages, or boot up and head for the hills. Happily, most of them concentrate on specific areas, so it's still possible to experience the unspoilt beauty that attracted the first travellers.

Most tourists flock to Windermere (largest and southernmost of the lakes), Ullswater, Derwentwater and the little town of Keswick in the north, before driving up the central valley of Langdale and taking in some of the prettier villages, such as Troutbeck, Hawkshead and Grasmere, once home to Wordsworth and his diarist sister, Dorothy.

The true Lakeland experience should include walking one of the superb horseshoe routes along the peaks and ridges, or escaping the crowds and visiting Crummock Water, Buttermere and lonely Wastwater, backed by the peaks of the Great Gable and Scafell, both excellent walking areas.

Scotland

Over the northern border lies Scotland, a remote country that packs some of Europe's wildest and most beautiful landscape into its 30,000 square miles (77,700 sq km). Its elegant capital is Edinburgh, its largest city Glasgow, and one fifth of its 5 million-strong population live in these two cities.

Unified politically with England since 1707, Scotland's relationship with the 'auld enemy' has always been problematical. Despite the establishment in 1999 of the devolved Scottish Parliament, Scots still view the 'big brother' south of the border with mixed feelings.

The country is defined by its scenery, a fabulous mix of mountain, loch and river in the north and green hills and fertile rolling farmland in the south, encircled by a 2,300-mile (3,680km) long coastline of immense splendour. Often shrouded in mist and driving rain, this landscape delivers the goods in terms of every cliché, from hills purple with heather to vivid autumn tints reflected in glassy lochs. Surrounded by this beauty, Scotland's grey stone towns and villages retain their own unique character, with a physical reality and spirit that's wholly different from urban life south of the border. Visitors revel in the great outdoors, the ancient castles, the whole tartan and whisky package – but increasingly outsiders are also beginning to see the reality of modern Scotland, a dynamic, self-assured country that's learnt to combine its heritage with a culture that looks firmly forward into the 21st century, and whose people are perhaps its greatest asset.

Orkney's Mainland contains the extensive remains of the Neolithic fishing and farming village of Skara Brae, built around 3,000BC. It came to light in 1850 when a fierce storm blew away the covering sands

133

Edinburgh

ABOVE *Carved from life, this statue near the Museum of Scotland commemorates Bobby, a Skye terrier who kept vigil for 14 years at his master's grave in Greyfriar's churchyard in the 1860s*

Scotland's capital is both a beautiful and historic city and a thriving, cosmopolitan centre, whose quality of life is rated the highest in Great Britain.

The city's history dates back to the Dark Ages, but it was only in the 15th century that it became the capital of Scotland. When James VI of Scotland became James I of England in 1603, Edinburgh was forced to accept the Union of the Crowns. A further blow was dealt to its prestige a century later, when the Union of the Parliaments in 1707 saw Scottish independence finally at an end. However, the guaranteed preservation of the national church and the Scottish legal and educational systems ensured the city never completely lost its national identity. Vindication came in the last years of the 20th century with the establishment of a Scottish parliament and a surge in national confidence.

Today, Edinburgh is a prosperous, slick and stylish city with a level of sophistication undreamt of even 20 years ago. The past is still highly visible: the castle still rises majestically over the tall tenements, narrow streets and dark vennels of the Old Town, while the broad streets and spacious squares of the New Town are still lined with gracious, classically-inspired buildings. Both neighbourhoods are packed with interest, though indubitably the big set-pieces of the castle and Holyrood draw the bigger crowds. All are in the Old Town, with the cobbled thoroughfare of the Royal Mile linking the 12th-century castle with the 16th-century royal palace of Holyrood, the Queen's official residence in Scotland.

The 200-year-old New Town, fronted by Princes Street, is an extraordinary development of crescents, squares, circuses and parks. These were raised during the late 18th and early 19th centuries, when shortage of space and cramped conditions saw the construction of an entirely new city area to the north of the castle. The New Town is home to art galleries and stylish shops, while theatres – at their most vibrant during the famous Edinburgh Festival in August – clubs and pubs are scattered throughout the city and its buzzing near neighbour and old port, Leith.

RIGHT *The spire of St Cuthbert's soars skywards against the backdrop of Edinburgh Castle. Its graveyard contains the tombs of landscape artist Alexander Nasmyth, John Smith, the inventor of logarithms, and writer Thomas de Quincy*

OPPOSITE *The annual Military Tattoo, running concurrently with the Edinburgh Festival, is staged against the spectacular backdrop of the castle. Displays by kilted mass pipe bands from around the world are among its most popular features*

BELOW LEFT *The classical philosophy behind the architecture of the New Town is epitomised by this doorway on Queen Street*

BELOW, BOTTOM *Views of the distinctive windows on the new Scottish Parliament building*

RIGHT *Fifty thousand tons of steel were used in the construction of the Forth Rail Bridge, built across the Firth of Forth to the northwest of Edinburgh, between 1883 and 1890 and a superb example of Victorian engineering*

Burns Country

The fertile west coast country of Ayrshire will forever be synonymous with Robert Burns (1759–1796), Scotland's much-loved national poet, whose verse continues to strike a note in people's hearts the world over.

Born in Alloway, his early years were marked by his father's poverty as a tenant farmer, an experience that gave him a life-long antipathy towards the land-owning classes. His first volume of poems was published in 1786 and was a best seller. Writing, however, didn't pay the bills and he was never able to abandon the day job, working throughout his short life as first a farmer, and later an exciseman.

Burns was a radical, a nationalist, a wit and a romantic. He was also a great womaniser, and many of his best-known songs celebrate his love for the fairer sex. He wrote always in his native Ayrshire Scots vernacular on familiar themes – celebrating, mourning and raging about life and the hand dealt to the common man. Worn out by hard labour and ill health, he died aged 37.

Southwest Scotland draws myriad visitors, who flock to his birthplace in Alloway, Ellisland Farm (where he lived from 1788–91) and his home and burial place in Dumfries.

RIGHT Robert Burns' parents' gravestone in the churchyard of ruined Alloway Kirk. Burns used the churchyard as the setting for part of his rollicking tale Tam o' Shanter, *the adventures of a drunk heading home from market*

LEFT Robert Burns' portrait appears everywhere in Ayrshire. The image on this pub sign is based on a 1786 portrait by Archibald Skirving

OPPOSITE Culzean Castle, overlooking the Firth of Clyde in Ayrshire, was built in 1777 by the great Scots architect Robert Adam on the site of an earlier Kennedy stronghold. The interior contains some of Adams' finest neoclassical designs

LEFT *The shiny Scottish Exhibition Centre, affectionately nicknamed the Armadillo, complements the 2001 Science Centre on the opposite bank of the Clyde*

ABOVE *The Charing Cross fountain epitomises solid Victorian values, hard work and prosperity – all contributed to Glasgow's industrial Golden Age*

Glasgow

Scotland's largest city, Glasgow has long since shaken off its downbeat image, the legacy, until the 1980s, of its industrial past. Chartered in 1175, the city evolved into an important university centre and port, and by the late 18th century its position on the River Clyde and easy access to the Lanarkshire coalfields had provided the impetus that transformed it into a Victorian industrial giant and the centre – until the 1930s – of British shipbuilding.

Mercantile and industrial wealth created the city, packed with solid and impressive Victorian buildings and home to a highly individualistic people, who retained their innate values throughout the hard times and depression of the late 20th century. The 1990s saw a complete turnaround, and Glaswegians have seen their city regain its role as a confident metropolis, noted for its unique combination of glitz and grime.

Glasgow has some of the finest 19th-century architecture in Britain, strikingly seen at its best in the art nouveau work of the architect and designer Charles Rennie Mackintosh (1868–1928). It also boasts a clutch of excellent museums, many of them sited around the turreted towers of the University in the city's West End. Elsewhere there's superb art at the eclectic Burrell Collection, while Glasgow's citizens and everyday life are celebrated at the People's Palace on Glasgow Green. The Glaswegians' love affair with 'the beautiful game' can be witnessed at Hampden Park, Scotland's national football stadium.

The heart of the city lies on the north bank of the Clyde, centred around the 19th-century municipal showcase of George Square and neighbouring Sauchiehall and Buchanan Streets, each a stone's throw from the yuppified grid of 18th-century warehouse streets now revived as the Merchant City.

West of here, peaceful Kelvingrove Park is home to galleries, museums and the university buildings, while to its south, on the riverside, Glasgow looks to the future through its ultra-modern, titanium-clad Science Centre, opened as a millennium project in 2001.

OPPOSITE *Everything in the Willow Tea Rooms, Sauchiehall Street – from the furniture, china and cutlery to the building itself – was designed by Charles Rennie Mackintosh. First opened in 1904, the tea rooms were restored and reopened in 1980*

Scotland

RIGHT *The huge expanse of Loch Lomond is dotted with islands which mark the Highland Line, a geological fault line that demarcates lowland and highland Scotland.*

BELOW *The panorama from Queen's View on Loch Tummel stretches to the northern limits of the Trossachs National Park*

OPPOSITE *The thistle, Scotland's floral emblem, blooms on roadsides, meadows and in the hills throughout the summer months*

Loch Lomond and the Trossachs

More than 70 per cent of Scotland's population live less than an hour's travel time away from Loch Lomond and the Trossachs, a hugely contrasting area that includes high mountains, lochs, rivers and woodlands. A national park was created in 2002, stretching from the southern end of Loch Lomond north to Tyndrum and Killin in Perthshire, and east from Callander almost to Loch Fyne.

The area is traversed by the West Highland Way, a spectacular long-distance footpath through some of Scotland's wildest beauty that follows old drove roads, military roads and even disused railways from the outskirts of Glasgow to Fort William in the north.

Most visitors stick to their cars for exploring the 720 square miles (1,865 sq km) of the park. The biggest attractions are Loch Lomond itself – the largest expanse of fresh water in Britain – and its attendant mountain, Ben Lomond, at 3,192ft/973m the most southerly of Scotland's Munros (the 284 Scottish mountains classified as standing over 3,000ft/914.4m). The western banks of Loch Lomond lie just 20 miles (32km) from the centre of Glasgow, drawing myriad weekend visitors. It's easy enough to escape the crowds on the eastern shore, however, and wooden ferries operate to the loch's scattering of islands from the village of Balmaha.

East of Loch Lomond lies the Trossachs, a magnificently diverse area of mountains, lochs and rivers that was first popularized by the writing of Sir Walter Scott (1771–1832) – his novel *Rob Roy* and long poem *The Lady of the Lake* were both set here. The real Rob Roy, a 17th-century outlaw with a reputation in Scotland as big as that of Robin Hood in England, was born at Loch Katrine and lived all his life in the Trossachs, turning from life as a respectable farmer to cattle stealing in 1712. His romanticised story, a dramatised illustration of the clash between Gaelic-speaking culture and organised Lowland society, which culminated in the Jacobite defeat at Culloden in 1746, draws thousands to the area.

The Trossachs' main towns are Callander, set on the banks of the River Teith at the south end of the Pass of Leny, and Aberfoyle, a sleepy little town that's packed with holidaymakers in summer. The latter is beautifully set near the forests of Loch Ard and the Queen Elizabeth Forest Park. Idyllic Loch Katrine is only accessible (as it has been since 1900) by a venerable steamer, the SS *Sir Walter Scott*, which chugs through some of the Trossach's most dramatic and attractive scenery.

North from here the country becomes wilder and less wooded with the start of the true Highlands. Roads are few in this remote region, whose main settlements are the villages of Crianlarich and Tyndrum. Tyndrum was the site of a mini-gold rush in the 19th century, and gold is still occasionally found in the surrounding hills.

East of Loch Lomond itself, Loch Long and the Argyll Forest Park on the Cowal peninsula offer another peaceful taste of this lovely area. Penetrated by the narrow sea lochs of Gairloch, Loch Long and Loch Fyne, the Cowal offers spectacular hills in the shape of the Arrochar Alps to the north of Loch Long, and utter tranquillity (and views to the lovely island of Arran) along the east shore of Loch Fyne, accessible via a narrow single-track road.

BELOW *The steep pass at the head of Glen Croe on the Cowal peninsula was named Rest and Be Thankful by exhausted early travellers*

OPPOSITE *Early, sharp frosts make autumn colours glow in the trees surrounding Loch Achray in the heart of the Trossachs*

Mull

The second largest of the Inner Hebrides, Mull is traditionally a crafting, fishing and distilling island. It lies across the Firth of Lorne from Oban, a busy harbour town on Scotland's West Highland coast. Its 19th-century population of 10,000 has dwindled to 2,500, but in Highland terms Mull is a success story, with a growing population of settlers from outside, drawn by the prospect of a peaceful way of life in unspoilt countryside.

Mull is an immensely varied island, with scenery that ranges from sometimes bleak, undulating tracts of moor and bog, to the grandeur of Ben More (3,169ft/966m),

an extinct volcano. The coastline is beautiful, particularly to the west, where white sand beaches around Calgary contrast with soaring cliffs at Loch na Keal, a deep indentation that almost bisects the island. North of here is the capital, Tobermory. The road south leads via pastoral Salen to Craignure, the main ferry port, and the castles of Torosay and Duart. From Craignure, a lonely road crosses the Ross of Mull to Fionnphort, the jumping off point for Iona and the magical island of Staffa, with its black basalt columns that inspired Felix Mendelssohn's overture *The Hebrides* (1829).

BELOW *The white sands of Calgary Bay are the finest on the island. Behind lie flower-rich machair and dunes, and there are spectacular views to Coll and Tiree*

OVER *Holidaymakers and pilgrims use the ferry service between Mull and the holy island of Iona – Iona's abbey buildings can be seen on the right in the background*

LEFT *Torosay Castle, a Scottish-Baronial pile near Craignure, is noted for its magnificent gardens, which include fine examples of 18th-century Venetian statuary, like this figure set in a niche in the garden walls*

INSIDE *The brightly coloured houses of Tobermory, founded in 1788 as a fishing port, cluster round a sheltered harbour in the north of the island. Tobermory plays a starring role in the children's TV story show* Balamory

Iona

Set like a jewel in clear blue waters, the holy island of Iona lies less than a mile off the southwestern tip of Mull. It was here, in 563, that St Colomba landed after his flight from Ireland, establishing a monastery whose monks spearheaded the conversion of pagan Scotland and much of northern England. The religion they taught was Celtic Christianity, and through the 6th and 7th centuries the monastery on Iona became a powerhouse of sacred learning and artistic endeavour. Its most famous illuminated manuscript, the *Book of Kells*, is on display in Trinity College, Dublin.

Viking raids and the relentless march of Rome led to the demise of the Celtic church, and by the 13th century Iona was part of mainstream Christianity, with a Benedictine monastery and Augustinian convent. Both were destroyed during the Reformation, along with all but three of the island's 360 magnificent Celtic crosses,

and Iona remained a backwater until 1899, when the abbey church was restored. In 1938 Glasgow minister George MacLeod established the Iona Community, which has evolved from a strictly male, Gaelic-speaking community into a vibrant, internationally renowned ecumenical society.

The heart of Iona is the sensitively restored Abbey, originally constructed by the Benedictines in the 13th century. It stands just north of the island's oldest building, St Oran's Chapel, and Reilig Odhráin (Oran's cemetery), an ancient burial ground said to contain the graves of 60 kings of Scotland, Ireland, Norway and France. Many of its exquisite carved stones have been moved for safe keeping, but St Martin's Cross, an 8th-century Celtic high cross, smothered in figurative carving, still stands beside the ancient cobbled Street of the Dead, which once led from the abbey down to the tiny village of Baile Mór.

ABOVE *The cloisters lie on the north side of Iona Abbey, where running water was available, rather than the traditional south side*

PAGE 146 *Iona's sparkling white sand beaches are formed by the grinding action of water on shells*

The East Neuk

From Largo Bay, on the north shore of the Firth of Forth, a string of coastal villages runs along the East Neuk, the name given to this southeastern corner of Fife. Historically prosperous from fishing and trade, it was aptly described in the 15th century by James II as 'the golden fringe on the beggar's mantle' of his poverty-stricken kingdom.

They still fish from the cosy stone harbours of Crail, Anstruther, Pittenweem, Elie and St Monans, five working villages that draw summer visitors in search of some of Scotland's best fish and seafood, good golf and wide sandy beaches. The crow-stepped gables and tiled roofs of these little settlements, perhaps Scotland's most appealing vernacular architecture, are an inheritance of medieval trading links with the Low Countries. The old houses range from tiny cottages lining the cobbled streets that run down to the harbours to grander merchants' houses. One of these, in Anstruther, houses the Scottish Fisheries Museum.

ABOVE *Tiny colour-washed houses with pan-tiled roofs line Culross's Back Causeway*

Culross

There's more history further up the Firth of Forth at Culross, the best-preserved 17th-century town in Scotland and once a major port with strong links to the Low Countries, as well as an early coal-mining centre.

This picturesque settlement, set right at the water's edge, has been beautifully restored by the National Trust for Scotland and is noted for its Dutch-influenced crow-stepped houses, cobbled streets with quaint names such as Stinking Wynd and Back Causeway, and above all, for Culross Palace. It's not a royal palace, but gets its name from the Latin word *palatium*, meaning hall, and was built in the 16th century by a rich coal merchant named George Bruce. Inside the mansion is a warren of panelled and painted small rooms and passages. Its dormer windows overlook a walled court, charmingly planted with a variety of historic species.

LEFT AND RIGHT *Before they are painted, the walls of the houses in Culross are covereed in a mix of fine gravel and cement, a process known as harling*

BELOW *Lobsters, crabs and crayfish decorate a house in Crail. The East Neuk is noted for the excellent shellfish caught off the rocky coastline*

St Andrews

North of Edinburgh, on the Fife coast, stands the historic city of St Andrews, once a great medieval shrine, and today famous as much for its role as the home of golf as that of Scotland's oldest university.

Legend tells of St Rule bringing St Andrews' bones here, and the ruins of the cathedral, founded in 1160 in honour of Scotland's patron saint, still dominate the east end of the town. Around it cluster an ancient clifftop castle and the buildings of the university. The town's main appeal lies to the west, where no fewer than seven golf courses spread out over the seaside links. Some of the world's most challenging golf is played out on the famous Old Course, founded in the 15th century.

Dundee

North of St Andrews, across the broad Firth of Tay, Dundee provides a remarkable contrast – a Victorian city which famously made its fortune on the three Js: jute, jam and journalism. Journalism survives, for the city is home to D C Thomson, creators of the *Beano* and *Dandy* comics, but modern Dundee is better known as an international centre for biotechnology and cancer research. Like Glasgow, Dundee is undergoing a renaissance, with its waterfront being redeveloped and a burgeoning cultural scene.

BELOW *From Dundee Law, a 571ft/174m high volcanic plug, there are wide views over the city to the waters of the Firth of Tay*

ABOVE *Captain Scott's ship* Discovery, *which carried his ill-fated expedition to the South Pole, was built in Dundee in 1901 and is now the focal point of the refurbished waterside*

LEFT *Golfers on the green of the 18th hole of the Old Course at St Andrews. The clubhouse, built in 1854, houses the world international governing body for the game*

Around Glencoe

Reached from the south across the desolate wilderness of Rannoch Moor, Glen Coe is shadowed by the mighty mountains of the Three Sisters. Scotland's most dramatic and evocative glen, it runs down to the sea at Loch Leven on Scotland's west coast. This spectacular mountain valley is enclosed between conical and rugged peaks, whose slopes, cascading with rock and scree, offer some of the country's most challenging rock and ice mountaineering.

The glen's atmosphere comes partly from its sheer physical presence, but mainly from its place in history as the site of the notorious 1692 massacre. Backed by the Hanoverian government, the Campbells, who had been quartered with the unruly MacDonalds, violated all rules of traditional Highland hospitality by slaughtering 40 of the Jacobite clan, sending the rest fleeing into a blizzard.

There are more Jacobite connections further north in Moidart, at Glenfinnan. This is where, in 1745, Prince Charles Edward Stuart raised his standard and gathered the clans at the start of his abortive uprising – a rebellion which was to end on the battlefield of Culloden and signal the final destruction of the Jacobite cause.

TOP *Regular steam services in summer run along the scenic line from Fort William to Mallaig, crossing the Glenfinnan Viaduct*

ABOVE *A column at Glenfinnan marks the spot where Prince Charlie raised his standard*

OPPOSITE *Winter on the Black Mount on Rannoch Moor, one of the most remote wildernesses in Britain. Red deer survive the harsh winters in these inhospitable conditions to provide some of Scotland's best stalking*

The Western Isles

ABOVE *Uig Sands on Lewis, the loveliest of the island's beaches. It was here the 12th-century Lewis Chessmen were discovered in 1831*

Across the stormy waters of the Minch, to the west of Skye, lies the windswept string of islands of the Outer Hebrides, or Western Isles. The 130-mile (208km) long archipelago runs from Lewis and Harris in the north, strongholds of the sternest form of Calvinism, to Catholic Uist and Barra in the south.

This is the Gaelic-speaking edge of Britain, an elemental land where the seas smash on huge cliffs or exhaust themselves on sweeping white-sand beaches. It's home to crofters, fishermen and weavers, most of whom live in the townships scattered throughout the islands and combine crofting – a unique form of land tenure and farming – with other local work.

Scenically, the islands are immensely different, ranging from barren peat moorland on Lewis through the bare peaks of Harris (separated only by its name) to the low-lying southern islands across the Sound of Harris. These – North Uist, Benbecula, South Uist and tiny

Barra – have vast sandy beaches backed by machair, a unique flowering, grassy strand that's home to some of Britain's shyest birds.

The small town of Stornoway on Lewis is the capital, with two-thirds of the Western Isles' population living to the northwest of here in a string of close-knit crofting communities on the Nis peninsula. Many are weavers, producing the hard-wearing and beautiful tweed that made Harris famous. Production is now centred on Lewis.

South of Nis is the stone circle of Calanais, a mysterious structure of nearly fifty stone monoliths dating to between 3,000 and 1,000BC. It is one of the most important prehistoric sites in Britain, second only to Stonehenge, Wiltshire.

To the south of Harris, the islands of North Uist, Benbecula and South Uist are linked by causeways, with access to Barra by ferry. From their western shores, a clear day brings views to remote St Kilda.

LEFT *In these treeless islands, peat has always been, and is still, the traditional fuel. Dug from the peat bogs during summer, it is stacked and dried for winter burning*

BELOW *Crofters once lived alongside their animals in these low, primitive dwellings, known as black houses from their smoke-blackened interiors – modernisation has bought chimneys and windows to this example on North Uist*

Skye

Skye's name comes from the Norse *ski*, meaning 'misty isle', and nothing could be more apt for this stunning island, the largest of the Inner Hebrides. Its mountains, often veiled in mist or wreathed in cloud, were formed by intense volcanic activity and glacial erosion, making its landscape among the most impressive in Britain. This is seen at its spectacular best in the Cuillins, jagged and menacing mountains to the west, but there's more drama in Trotternish to the north, where craggy rock formations, formed of residual basalt, rise up in the eerie landscape of the Quiraing.

Skye was annexed by Norway in the 8th century and later blighted by the Clearances, when the local clans were cleared to make way for the more profitable sheep. In the 19th century thousands sailed to the New World, and their descendants still return to seek their roots in place such as Dunvegan, a 15th-century castle and seat of the Macleods, and the crofting townships around Portree. This is the island's capital, a snug fishing harbour, lined with colour-washed houses, on the east coast.

From here, the road runs south to Kyleakin and the road bridge that now links Skye with the mainland.

ABOVE *The mountains of the Red Cuillin from the beach at Elgol, a tiny settlement reached via a tortuous 14-mile (22.5km) single-track road*

FAR LEFT *The Old Man of Storr in the Quiraing. The rocks are formed of volcanic lava*

LEFT *The monument to Jacobite heroine Flora MacDonald – who helped Bonnie Prince Charlie to escape after Culloden – in the cemetery at Kilmuir. Thousands attended her funeral in 1790, forming a mile-long procession*

Index

A

Abbotsbury Swannery **46**
Aberfoyle 144
Adam, Robert 49, 138
Alfred, King 41
Alloway 138
Alnwick 126
Anglesey 80–1, **80–1**
Anning, Mary 45
Anstruther 148
Arthur, King 41, 84
Ashbourne 114
Aysgarth 118

B

Bakewell 112, **112**, 115
Bala Lake 78
Bamburgh Castle 126, **126**
Bath 48–9, **48–9**, 99
Beachy Head 22, **23**, 32
Beaumaris 81, **81**
Benbecula 154
Birmingham 87
Black Mountains 68, **68**, 88
Blaenau Ffestiniog 75, 76, 78
Blenheim Palace **96**, 99
Bodiam Castle 30, **30**
Bournemouth 46
Brecon 70
Brecon Beacons 65, 68–71, **68–71**
Brighton 28–9, **28–9**
Bristol 41
Brixham 60, **61**
Brown, Capability 96, 115
Bulwer-Lytton, Edward 31

Burford 96
Burns, Robert 138, **138**
Buttermere 130, **130–1**
Buxton 112, **112**

C

Caesar, Julius 21
Calanais 154
Callander 143, 144
Cambridge 87, 102, **102–3**
Canterbury 21, **24**, 25
Cardiff 65, **65**, 66–7, 70
Carroll, Lewis 83
Castel Dinas **85**
Castleton 112
Celts 41, 73, 147
Central England 86–109
Charles Edward Stuart, Prince 152, 157
Chatsworth 115, **115**
Chaucer, Geoffrey 25
Chesil Beach 45–6
Chipping Camden 96, **96–7**, 99
Chipping Norton 96
Chitty Chitty Bang Bang 87
Church Stretton 88
Cirencester 96
Cleveland Way 122, 124
Clovelly 60, **60**
Coleridge, Samuel Taylor 50
Constable, John 128
Conwy **82**, 83, **83**
Cook, James 124
Cotswold Way 99
Cotswolds 87, 96–9, **96–9**

Crail 148, **149**
Craster 126
Crickhowell 68, 70
Crome, John 106
Cromwell, Oliver 105
Cuckmere Haven 22
Cuillins 156, **156–7**
Culloden 144
Culross 148, **149**
Culzean Castle **139**

D

Darby, Abraham 92
Dartmoor 41, 56–9, **56–9**
Derwentwater **128–9**, 130
Devonshire, Dukes of 115
Dilwyn **88**
Discovery, SS **151**
Donne, John 12
Dover 21, **24–5**, 25
Doyle, Conan 57
druids 81
Dumfries 138
Dundee 150, **150–1**
Dunkery Beacon 50, **51**
Dunstanburgh Castle 126

E

Eastbourne **20–1**
Eden Project **54**
Edinburgh 133, 134–7, **134–7**
Edward I 27, 81, 83
Edward VII 19
Elie 148
Elizabeth II 19, 38, 134
Ellesmere Canal **84**
Encaenia **94**
Ethelbert, King 25
Exmoor 41, 50–1, **50–1**

F

Ffestiniog Railway 78, **78, 79**
Fort William 143, 152
Forth Rail Bridge **136–7**
Foster, Norman 15
Fyne, Loch 143, 144

G

Gainsborough, Thomas 104
George III 19
George IV 29, 108
Gibbons, Grinling 12, 38
Glasgow 133, **140–1**, 143, 150
Glastonbury Tor **40–1**
Glencoe 152
Glendwr, Owain 76
Glenfinnan 152, **152**
Golden Hind 61
Gower Peninsula 67, **67**
Great Gable 130
Great Orme 83
Grosmont 124

H

Hadrian's Wall **110–1**
Hardraw Force 118
Harris 154
Harvard, John 100
Hawkesmoor, Nicholas 94, 96
Hay-on-Wye 68, 70
Heacham **108–9**
Heligan, Lost Gardens of 54, **55**
Henry II 25, 38
Henry IV 102
Henry VII 35

Henry VIII 35
Hepworth, Barbara 62, **63**
Holkham 108, **109**
Holy Island *see* Lindisfarne
Holyhead 81, 84
Horning **106–7**
Housman, A E 88
Hutton-le-Hole 124

I

Ingleborough 118
Iona 146–7, **146–7**
Ironbridge 92, **92–3**

James I 134
James II 148
James VI of Scotland 134
James, Henry 27
Jekyll, Gertrude 31
Jurassic Coast 45

K

Katrine, Loch 144
Kelmscot 99, **99**
Kendal **130**
Keswick 129, 130
Killin 143
Kilnsey Crag **118**
Knebworth 31, **31**

L

Lake District 111, 128–31, **128–31**
Land's End 52
Lavenham 104, **104**
Leach, Bernard 62
Leeds 111
Lennon, John **90**

Lewes 32, **32**
Lewis 154
Lindisfarne **126**
Liverpool 90–1, **90–1**
Llandudno 83, **83**
Llanfair PG 81
Llangollen 78, 84–5,
84–5
Llyn Cwm Llwch **68**
Llywelyn ap Gruffyd 76
Lomond, Loch **142**, 143
London 8–19, 21, 29,
84, 100
Long Mynd 88, **89**
Lost Gardens *see* Heligan
Ludlow 88, **88**
Lulworth Cove **44–5**, 46
Lundy 60
Lutyens, Edwin 31, 126

M

MacDonald, Flora 157
Mackintosh, Charles
Rennie 141
Malhamdale 116, 118
Malverns 87
Manchester 111
Marches 65, 87, 88
Marlborough, Duke of
96, 99
Menai Straits 81
Mendelssohn, Felix 12
Merthyr Tydfil 70
Millennium Centre,
Cardiff **64–5**
Monmouth and Brecon
Canal 70, **70**
Moreton-in-Marsh
96, **99**
Morris, William 99
Mull 147

N

Nash, John 10, 19, 29

Nelson, Admiral Lord
Horatio 10, 12, 35
New Forest 21, 36–7,
36–7
Newcastle upon Tyne
111, 126
Nicolson, Ben 62
Norfolk Broads 106,
106–7
North York Moors 111,
122–5, **122–5**
North York Moors
Railway 124
**Northern England
111–131**
Norwich 106, **106**

O

Orkney **132–3**
Oxford 87, 94–5,
94–5, 102

P

Peak District 111, 112–5,
112–5
Pembroke 72–3, **72–3**
Pen y Fan **68**
Pennine Way 118
Pennines 116
Pen-y-Ghent 118
Percy family 126
Pickering 124
Pittenweem 148
Plymouth 41
Pontcysyllte Aqueduct **84**
Porlock 50
Porthmadog **74–5**,
75, 78
Portmeirion **74**, 75
Portsmouth 21, 34–5, **35**
Postbridge **56**
Preseli 42, 73
Princetown 57
Pugin, Augustus 10

Q

Queen Elizath Forest
Park 144
Quiraing 156, **157**

R

Rannoch Moor 152, **153**
Rest and Be Thankful **144**
Rhossili 67
Richmond 116–8
Rievaulx Abbey 122
Robin Hood's Bay **123**
Romney Marshes 27
Roy, Rob 144
Rutland, Duke of 115
Rye 26–7, **26–7**

S

Saffron Waldon 104, **105**
Scafell 128, 130
Scara Brae **132–3**
Scotland 132–57
Scott, Robert Falcon 151
Scott, Walter 144
Scottish Parliament 133,
134, **136**
Settle 116, **116–7**
Sgwd-yr-Eira falls **71**
Shakespeare, William
87, 100
Sheffield 111
Shrewsbury 92
Skye 154, 156–7
Snowdon Mountain
Railway 78
Snowdon, Mount 76,
78, **78**
Snowdonia 65, 76–8,
76–8, 84
Somerset Levels 41
South Downs 21, 22,
32, **32–3**
South Downs Way 22, 32
Southeast England 20–39

Southwest Coast Path
45, **47**, 50
**Southwest England
41–63**
St Andrews 150, **150–1**
St Augustine 25
St Columba 147
St David's 73, **73**
St Ives 62, **62–3**
St Kilda 154
St Thomas à Becket 25
Staithes 124
Stoker, Bram 124
Stonehenge 41, 42, **42–3**,
73, 154
Stourhead 54, **54–5**
Stratford-upon-Avon
87, **100–1**
Swaledale 116
Swansea 65, **66,** 67

T

Telford, Thomas 81, 83, 84
Thomas, Dylan **66**
Tiger Bay 66
Torquay 52, **53**
Tretower Court 70
Trossachs **141–5**, 144
Tryfan **76–7**
Tummel, Loch **142–3**
Turville **86–7**
Tyndrum 143, 144

U

Uist 154, **154–5**
UNESCO World
Heritage Sites 42,
48, 92

V

Valley of the Rocks **50**
Vanbrugh, John 96
Victoria, Queen 19
Victory, HMS **34–5**, 35

W

Waen Rydd **68–9**
Wainwath Falls **119**
Wales 64–85
Wallis, Alfred 62
Warkworth 126
Wellington, Duke of 12
Welsh Assembly 67
Wensleydale 118
West Highland Way 143
Weymouth 45, **45**, 46,
52, **52–3**
Wharfedale 116, **118, 119**
Whistler, Rex 81
Whitby **122–3**, 124
Widecombe-in-the-
Moor 57
William I 9, 21, 32,
35, 38
William III 60
Williams-Ellis, Clough
75
Willow Tea Rooms **140**
Windermere 130
Windsor Castle 21,
38, **38–9**
Wolsey, Cardinal 94
Woolf, Virginia 62
Wordsworth, William
128, 130
Worm's Head 67
Wren, Christopher
12, 94

Y

Ynys Môn *see* Anglesey
York 120, **120–1**
Yorkshire Dales 111,
116–9, **116–9**

Acknowledgements

The Automobile Association would like to thank the following photographers and libraries for their assistance in the preparation of this book
Abbreviations are as follows: AA = AA World Travel Library, t (top), b (bottom), c (centre), l (left), r (right)

1 AA/Richard Turpin; 2/3 AA/Ian Burgum; 4/5 AA/S & O Mathews; 8/9 AA/Rick Strange; 10/11 AA/Jenny McMillan; 11t AA/Wyn Voysey; 12 AA/Max Jourdan; 12/13 AA/Rick Strange; 14 AA/Clive Sawyer; 15t AA/Max Jourdan; 15br P. Narayan/age fotostock/Superstock; 16t AA/Paul Kenward, a Registered trade mark of Transport for London; 16b AA/Max Jourdan; 17 AA/Max Jourdan; 18/19 AA/Max Jourdan; 19 AA/Simon McBride; 20/21 AA/John Miller; 22 AA/John Miller; 23 AA/John Miller; 24t AA/Malcolm Birkitt; 24/25 AA/Malcolm Birkitt; 26 AA/John Miller; 27 AA/Wyn Voysey; 28/29 AA/Wyn Voysey; 29t AA/Derek Forss; 29b AA/John Miller; 30 AA/John Miller; 31l AA/Caroline Jones; 31r AA/Malcolm Birkitt; 32 AA/John Miller; 32/33 AA/John Miller; 34 AA/Peter Baker; 35l AA/S & O Mathews; 35r Paul Seheult/Eye Ubiquitous; 36 AA/Wyn Voysey; 37 AA/Wyn Voysey; 38t AA/Caroline Jones; 38b AA/Wyn Voysey; 38/39 AA/Wyn Voysey/ THE DEAN AND CANONS OF WINDSOR; 40/41 AA/Caroline Jones; 42/43 AA/Eric Meacher; 43 AA/Eric Meacher; 44/45 AA/Max Jourdan; 45tc AA/Max Jourdan; 45tr AA/Richard Ireland; 46t AA/Richard Ireland; 46b AA/Max Jourdan; 47 AA/Max Jourdan; 48tl AA/Eric Meacher; 48/49 AA/Caroline Jones; 49tr AA/Caroline Jones; 49br AA/Caroline Jones; 50 AA/Caroline Jones; 51 AA/Steve Day; 52t AA/Max Jourdan; 52/53 AA/Max Jourdan; 53t AA/Caroline Jones; 54bl AA/Rupert Tenison; 54/55 AA/Wyn Voysey; 55b AA/Caroline Jones; 56 AA/Peter Baker; 57t AA/Peter Baker; 57b AA/Robert Mort; 58/59 AA/Andrew Lawson; 60 AA/Caroline Jones; 61l AA/Caroline Jones; 61r AA/Caroline Jones; 62 AA/Caroline Jones; 63t Ellen Rooney/Robert Harding; 63bl AA/Rupert Tenison; 63br AA/Roger Moss; 64/65 Billy Stock/Photolibrary Wales; 66tr Jeff Morgan/ Photolibrary Wales; 66c AA/Caroline Jones; 66bl AA/Caroline Jones; 67 AA/Ian Burgum; 68l AA/Ian Burgum; 68/69 AA/Ian Burgum; 70 AA/Nick Jenkins; 71 AA/Ian Burgum; 72 AA/Jeff Beazley; 73t AA/Ronnie Weir; 73b AA/Nick Jenkins; 74 David Williams/Photolibrary Wales; 74/75 AA/Ian Burgum; 76/77 AA; 78cl AA/Pat Aithie; 78b AA/Wyn Voysey; 79 AA/Pat Aithie; 80/81 AA/Derek Croucher; 81tr AA/Pat Aithie; 82 AA/Caroline Jones; 83tr AA/Caroline Jones; 83b AA/Caroline Jones; 84t AA/Nick Jenkins; 84b AA/Wyn Voysey; 84/85 AA/Nick Jenkins; 86/87 AA/Derek Forss; 88t AA/Wyn Voysey; 88b AA/Ian Burgum; 89 AA/Mike Haywood; 90tl Michael Jenner/Robert Harding; 90b Suzanne & Nick Geary/Getty Images; 91 Guy Woodland; 91br Guy Woodland; 92tl AA/Mike Haywood; 92tc AA/Mike Haywood; 92/93 AA/Mike Haywood; 94t AA/Kenya Doran; 94b AA/Andrew Lawson; 95 AA/Caroline Jones; 96tl AA/Caroline Jones; 96/97 AA/Steve Day; 98 AA/Steve Day; 99t AA/Kenya Doran; 99b AA/Steve Day; 100 AA/Hugh Palmer; 101 AA/Hugh Palmer; 102 Britain on View www.britainonview.com; 103 AA/Malcolm Birkitt; 104 AA/Tom Mackie; 105tl AA/ Linda Whitwam; 105tr AA/Linda Whitwam; 105b AA/Chris Coe; 106tl AA/Tom Mackie; 106b AA/Tom Mackie; 106/107 AA/Adrian Baker; 107tr AA/Chris Coe; 108/109 AA/Tom Mackie; 109b AA/Tom Mackie; 110/111 AA/Jeff Beazley; 112tl AA/A J Hopkins; 112b AA/Peter Baker; 113 AA/Jeff Beazley; 114l AA/Andy Midgley; 114/115 AA/Andy Tryner; 115br AA/A J Hopkins; 116tl David Tarn; 116/117 AA/John Mottershaw; 118 AA/John Morrison; 119t AA/David Tarn; 119b AA/David Tarn; 120t AA/Rich Newton; 120b AA/Pete Bennett; 121 AA/Rich Newton; 122/123 AA/Linda Whitwam; 123t AA/John Morrison; 124 AA/John Morrison; 125 AA/John Morrison; 126 Laurie Campbell; 127 AA/Cameron Lees; 128/129 AA/Steve Day; 129b AA/E A Bowness; 130tl AA/Pete Bennett; 130/131 AA/Tom Mackie; 132/133 AA/Stephen Whitehorne; 134t AA/Ken Paterson; 134b AA/Jonathan Smith; 135 AA/Jonathan Smith; 136cl AA/Jonathan Smith; 136cr Scottish Parliamentary Corporate Body 2005; 136b Scottish Parliamentary Corporate Body 2005; 137 AA/Jonathan Smith; 138t AA/Ken Paterson; 138b AA/Sue Anderson; 139 AA/Sue Anderson; 140 AA/Stephen Whitehorne; 141tl AA/Stephen Whitehorne; 141tr AA/Stephen Gibson; 142t AA/Steve Day; 142/143 AA/Steve Day; 143tr AA/Ken Paterson; 144 AA/Ken Paterson; 145 AA; 146 AA/Derek Forss; 147 AA/Richard Elliot; 148 AA/Jonathan Smith; 149tl AA/Jonathan Smith; 149tr AA/Jim Carnie; 149b AA/Steve Day; 150bl AA/Jonathan Smith; 150/151 AA/Stephen Whitehorne; 151tr AA/Jonathan Smith; 152t AA/Steve Day; 152b AA/Stephen Whitehorne; 153 AA/Sue Anderson; 154tl AA/Stephen Whitehorne; 154/155b AA/Robert Eames; 155t AA/Richard Elliot; 156/157t AA/Stephen Whitehorne; 157bl AA/Stephen Whitehorne; 157br AA/Alan Grierley

GATEFOLDS
Ascot: Royals - John Stillwell/PA/Empics; Crowd scene - Martin Cushen/Action Plus; Horses racing - Julian Herbert/Getty Images; Lady in hat - Mike Egerton/Empics

Liverpool: Liverpool Metropolitan Cathedral - Paul McMullin/www.liverpoolimages.co.uk; Albert Docks at night - Paul McMullin/www.liverpoolimages.co.uk; Waterfront - www.vkguy.co.uk; Football fans - Scott Barbour/Getty Images

Newcastle: Sage Centre - Graeme Peacock; Naked people - Mark Pinder; Night view - Graeme Peacock; Angel of the North - Graeme Peacock

Mull: Calgary Bay – AA/Stephen Whitehorne; Boat – AA/Richard Elliot; Tobermory – AA/Stephen Whitehorne; Torosay – AA/Richard Elliot

FRONT COVER: Edmund Nagele Photography
BACK COVER: AA/ Cameron Lees

Every effort has been made to trace the copyright holders, and we apologise in advance for any unintentional errors or omissions. We would be pleased to apply any corrections in any following edition of this publication.